TOP 10
BEIJING

ANDREW HUMPHREYS

EYEWITNESS TRAVEL

915.11
BEI
2013
+ Map

$14

B+T

Left **Tian'an Men** Center **Temple of Heaven** Right **Summer Palace**

x

LONDON, NEW YORK,
MELBOURNE, MUNICH AND DELHI
www.dk.com

Produced by Brazil Street

Printed and bound in China by Leo Paper Products Ltd

First American Edition, 2007

13 14 15 16 10 9 8 7 6 5 4 3 2 1

Published in the United States by DK Publishing, 375 Hudson Street, New York, New York 10014

Reprinted with revisions 2009, 2011, 2013

Copyright 2007, 2013 © Dorling Kindersley Limited, London. A Penguin Company

Published in the UK by Dorling Kindersley Limited.

A catalog record for this book is available from the Library of Congress.

ISSN 1479-344X
ISBN: 978 0 75669 675 7

Within each Top 10 list in this book, no hierarchy of quality or popularity is implied. All 10 are, in the editor's opinion, of roughly equal merit.

Floors are referred to throughout in accordance with British usage: ie the "first floor" is the floor above ground level.

MIX
Paper from
responsible sources
FSC™ C018179
www.fsc.org

Contents

Beijing's Top 10

The information in this DK Eyewitness Top 10 Travel Guide is checked regularly.
Every effort has been made to ensure that this book is as up-to-date as possible at the time of going to press. Some details, however, such as telephone numbers, opening hours, prices, gallery hanging arrangements and travel information are liable to change. The publishers cannot accept responsibility for any consequences arising from the use of this book, nor for any material on third party websites, and cannot guarantee that any website address in this book will be a suitable source of travel information. We value the views and suggestions of our readers very highly. Please write to: Publisher, DK Eyewitness Travel Guides, Dorling Kindersley, 80 Strand, London WC2R 0RL, UK, or email: travelguides@dk.com.

11–13

Left **Foil-baked fish, Han Cang** Center **Mesh bar, Sanlitun** Right **Mahjong players, Hou Hai**

Left **Forbidden City** Right **Lama Temple**

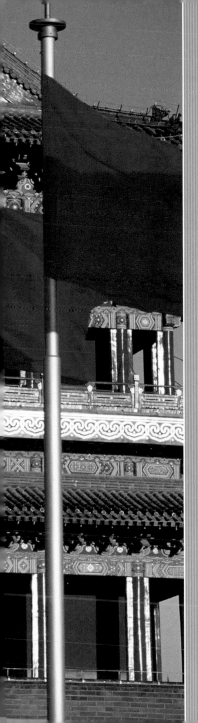

BEIJING'S
TOP 10

BEIJING'S TOP 10

TOP10 Beijing's Highlights

At the heart of Beijing is tradition, given physical form in the mighty Forbidden City, from where successive imperial dynasties have ruled since the 15th century. Neighboring Tian'an Men Square is the China of recent history, of red-flag socialism and Mao. But this is also a city on the move, as an all-pervading spirit of change makes Beijing the most 21st-century of capitals.

Forbidden City 1
So called because at one time only members of the imperial court were allowed inside, this is one of the largest and greatest palace complexes ever built *(see pp8–11)*.

Temple of Heaven 2
Originally the venue for annual winter solstice sacrifices, which were performed by successive emperors to ensure ample harvests, the temple remains Beijing's most recognizable icon *(see pp12–13)*.

Tian'an Men Square 3
The world's largest public square is not pretty, but it is surrounded by august cultural and political institutions, and it is also the final resting place of Chairman Mao Zedong *(see pp14–15)*.

Lama Temple 4
The largest and most spectacular of the city's temples is a working lamasery, home to monks from Mongolia and Tibet *(see pp16–17)*.

Bei Hai Park 5
The most beautiful of Beijing's many city parks is laid out around a central lake, first dug out in the 12th century, with the excavated earth used to create a central island. The famed Kublai Khan ruled his empire from a palace here *(see pp18–19)*.

Map labels:
ANDING MEN XI DAJIE
TUCIUOLU DAJIE
GUOWANG HUTONG
JIUOU DONG
6 Hou Hai
Qian Hai
DI'AN MEN XI DAJIE
DI'AN MEN WAI DAJIE
Bei Hai Park 5
XISI BEI DAJIE
DESHENGMEN NEIDAJIE
Bei Hai
Dian Men
Jing Shan Park
XI'AN MEN DAJIE
WEN/JIN JIE
JING SHAN QIAN JIE
Zhong Hai
1 Forbidden City
XIDAN BEI DAJIE
FUYOU JIE
NANCHANG JIE
NANCHIZI DAJIE
Nán Hǎi
XUANWU MEN NEI DAJIE
BEI XINHUA JIE
XI CHANG'AN JIE
XUANWU MEN DONG DAJIE
QIAN MEN XI DAJIE
3 Tian'an Men Square
QIAN MEN DAJIE
NAN XINHUA JIE
LUOMASHI DAJIE
ZHUSHIKOU XI DAJIE
ZHUSHIKOU
TIANQIAO NAN DAJIE
ZHUSHIKOU

Previous pages **Red flags flying on Tian'an Men Square**

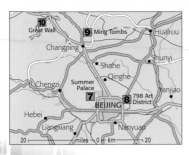

Hou Hai

By day visitors take rickshaw tours around the back lanes for a glimpse of fast-disappearing old Beijing; by night, attention shifts to the area's lakeside bars and restaurants *(see pp20–21)*.

Summer Palace

Beijing summers are unbearably hot, so the imperial court would exchange the Forbidden City for this semi-rural retreat with its ornate pavilions, gardens, and temples, ranged around the cool expanse of Kunming Lake *(see pp22–3)*.

798 Art District

When former electronic components factory 798 became a venue for cutting-edge contemporary art it kick-started a neighborhood trend for converting industrial spaces into galleries and chic cafés and bars *(see pp24–5)*.

Ming Tombs

Thirty miles (45 km) northwest of Beijing is the vast burial site of 13 of China's 16 Ming emperors. One of the underground tombs can be visited but most impressive of all is the Sacred Way, with its 12 pairs of stone guardians *(see pp26–7)*.

Great Wall

"Great" is something of an understatement; the wall is nothing less than spectacular. Clamber up the perilously sloping carriageways to one of the crowning watchtowers and the experience is also quite literally breathtaking *(see pp28–9)*.

Forbidden City

Officially known as the Palace Museum, this magnificent complex is a grand monument to the 24 emperors who ruled from its halls over a period of almost 500 years. The symbolic center of the Chinese universe, the palace was the exclusive domain of the imperial court from its completion in 1420 until the last of the emperors was forced to abdicate at the beginning of the 20th century. The modern world intruded in 1949, when the public were finally admitted through the palace gates.

Bronze guardian lion

Glazed panel with lotus and mandarin ducks

🍴 There are various snack kiosks near the ticket office, and one restaurant inside the Forbidden City.

✪ Most visitors buy their tickets at the Meridian Gate, but to avoid the lengthy queues you could enter the Forbidden City from the north via the Gate of Divine Prowess, and visit in reverse.

North of Tian'an Men Square • Map L3
• 8500 7420
• Subway: Tian'an Men West or Tian'an Men East
• Open: Apr 1–Oct 31 8:30am–5pm daily. Nov 1–Mar 31 8:30am–4:30pm daily. Last entry one hr before closing
• Admission: Apr 1–Oct 31 ¥60. Nov 1–Mar 31 ¥40. There are additional charges for certain halls
• Audio guides are available for ¥40 (plus ¥100 deposit)
• www.dpm.org.cn

Top 10 Features

1. Meridian Gate
2. Golden Water
3. Gate of Supreme Harmony
4. Hall of Supreme Harmony
5. Hall of Preserving Harmony
6. Gate of Heavenly Purity
7. Inner Court
8. Imperial Garden
9. Western Palaces
10. Eastern Palaces

1 Meridian Gate
In Chinese it is the Wu Men. This is the traditional entrance to the palaces. From the balcony *(above)* the emperor would review his armies and perform ceremonies marking the start of the new lunar year.

2 Golden Water
Five marble bridges, symbolizing the five cardinal virtues of Confucianism, span the Golden Water, which flows from west to east in a course designed to resemble the jade belt worn by the court officials.

3 Gate of Supreme Harmony
The fourth and final great gate *(below)* gives access into the Outer Court, the heart of the Forbidden City. The gate is guarded by two large bronze lions, classic imperial symbols of power and dignity. The lion on the right *(top)* is the male; the one on the left with a cub under its foot is the female.

Hall of Supreme Harmony 4

Raised on a triple tier of marble terraces, this largest of halls houses a sandalwood throne *(right)*, used in the coronations of 24 emperors.

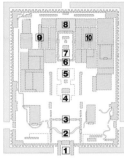

Hall of Preserving Harmony 5

The most spectacular aspect of this hall is the great carved ramp on the north side, sculpted with dragons and clouds, and made from a single piece of marble weighing more than 200 tons.

Gate of Heavenly Purity 6

The only building *(above)* in the whole palace not to have been burnt down at least once, and thus the oldest hall of all. It is the boundary between the Outer Court (official) and Inner Court (private).

Inner Court 7

The Inner Court *(left)* is more intimate than the formal Outer Court, because this is where the emperor, empress, and the many concubines actually lived.

The Last Emperor

Pu Yi, ascended the throne at the age of three in 1908, but his brief reign was brought to an early end in 1912 by a new Republican government. The young ex-emperor continued to live in the Forbidden City until ejected in 1924. He was later imprisoned under the Communists, until Mao granted him amnesty in 1959. He died in 1967, after working for seven years as a gardener.

Western Palaces 9

Much of the western flank of the complex is off limits, but some of the halls neighboring the Inner Court are visitable, including the Palace of Eternal Spring, where *trompe-l'oeil* paintings at the ends of passageways make them appear infinitely extended.

Eastern Palaces 10

East of the Inner Court are smaller halls where the emperor's harem lived. Also here is the well down which the Empress Cixi *(see p23)* had her nephew's favorite concubine thrown.

Imperial Garden 8

The emperor Qianlong wrote that, "Every ruler, when he has finished his public duties, must have a garden in which he can stroll, and relax his heart" This formal garden, the oldest in the Forbidden City, has two beautiful pavilions *(above)*.

Beijing's Top 10

For more places of interest in the vicinity of the Forbidden City
See pp66–9

Left **Nine-dragon screen** Right **Imperial throne**

⊤₀⌐10 Forbidden City Collections

1 Musical instruments

In true imperial fashion, the more lavish the musical entertainment, the more glory it reflected on the emperor. Court musicians used gongs of all sizes and *guqins* (zithers), wooden flutes, and heavy bronze bells adorned with dragons, as well as the unusual *sheng*, a Sherlock Holmes-style pipe with reeds of different lengths sprouting from the top. The collection is displayed in the Silver Vault of the Imperial Palace, on the west side of the Outer Court.

Butterfly brooch

2 Scientific instruments

Enlightened Qing emperor Kangxi (1654–1722) appointed Europeans as court officials, and instructed his imperial workshops to copy Western scientific instruments. These included the first calculator, astronomical and drawing tools, sun dials, moon dials, and a special table with measurements and scientific notations scratched on each side leaf, made especially for the imperial studies. The instruments are part of the Imperial Treasures of the Ming and Qing Dynasties exhibit, on the west side of the Inner Court.

3 Stone drums

The Hall of Moral Cultivation holds the palace's collection of stone drums. These are enormous tom-tom shaped rocks that bear China's earliest stone inscriptions dating back to 374 BC. These ideographic carvings are arranged in four-character poems, which commemorate the glorious pastureland and successful animal husbandry made possible by the Emperor Xiangong's benevolence.

4 Jewelry

Also in the Hall of Moral Cultivation are three of the six halls of jewelry (head north for rooms four through six), including the only hall to display actual jewelry rather than agate cups or jade sculpture. Hall number three has thick jade rings, lapis lazuli court beads, elaborate headdresses made of gold filigree phoenixes, and surprisingly, jadeite Christian rosary beads.

5 Beijing Opera

The pleasantly named Pavilion of Cheerful Melodies sports a three-story stage large enough to accommodate one thousand actors. It was once rigged with pulleys and trapdoors to create dramatic entrances for supernatural characters. The exhibits include a behind-the-scenes model stage, as well as costumes, instruments, scripts, and cast lists. There are screens showing reconstructions of old court performances.

Share your travel recommendations on traveldk.com

6 Jade

The Hall of Quintessence was once where dowager empresses went to die; it now exhibits jade artifacts spanning thousands of years. Pieces range from simple cups and ladles to enormous and intricate sculptures of Buddhas in traditional scenic settings. The Chinese considered working this "hard" stone a metaphor for character development and the pursuit of perfection.

7 Daily life of the concubines

Every three years, court officials would select girls between the ages of 13 and 17 to join the eight ranks of imperial concubines. The Yonghe Pavilion exhibits clothing, games, herbal medicine, and a food distribution chart relating to the young imperial consorts, as well as the all-important "wedding night bed," which is covered in a richly embroidered red silk decorated with Chinese mythological symbols.

Imperial wedding bed

8 Clocks and watches

Arguably the finest of the many and varied palace collections, the clocks and watches fill the Fengxian Pavilion in the southeastern corner of the eastern Inner Court. The size and creativity involved in some of the pieces – which are primarily European – is astonishing. One particularly inventive model has an automaton clad in European dress frantically writing eight Chinese characters on a scroll, which is being unrolled by two other mechanical figures.

Ornate carriage clock

9 Ceramics

In a ceramic salute to the Silk Road, several linked halls around the Inner Court display tomb figurines from the Sui (581–618) and Tang (618–906) dynasties. Still caked with earth, statues range from six inches to three feet (15 cm to 1m) in height, and depict overweight court ladies, Buddhas on elephants, and floppy-humped camels. A film offers some background on the pottery finds.

10 Empress Cixi

The Xianfu Pavilion is a memorial to the Empress Cixi's devious rise to power *(see p23)*, as well as to the great lady's imperial extravagances, which so nearly crippled her country. Clothes, jewelry, embroidered socks, imported perfume, jade and ivory chopsticks, and pictures of clothes and food form the bulk of the exhibits. There are also examples of the empress's calligraphic skills in the form of painted wall hangings.

 For more Beijing museums **See pp42–3**

⑩ Temple of Heaven (Tiantan)

It was here that the emperor would make sacrifices and pray to heaven and his ancestors at the winter solstice. As the Son of Heaven, the emperor could intercede with the gods on behalf of his people and pray for a good harvest. Off-limits to the common people during the Ming and Qing dynasties, the temple complex is now fully open to the public and attracts thousands of visitors daily, including many local Chinese who come to enjoy the large and pleasant park in which the monuments are set.

Triple gate for emperor, officials, and gods

🍜 There are several small snack kiosks in the park grounds.

✪ Just as fascinating as exploring the temple is observing the great numbers of Chinese who come to the park to dance, exercise, sing opera, play games of cards and mahjong, and fly kites.

Tian Tan Dong Lu (East Gate), Chongwen
• *Map F6*
• *6702 8866*
• *Subway:*
Tian Tan Dong Men
• *Park open: 6am–10pm daily. Temple open: Mar–Jun: 8am–5:30pm; Jul–Oct: 8am–6pm; Nov–Feb: 8am–5pm*
• *Admission to temple: ¥35. Admission to park: ¥10. Audio guides are available for ¥40, plus deposit of ¥100*
• *www.tiantanpark.com*

Top 10 Features

1. Hall of Prayer for Good Harvests
2. Painted Caisson Ceiling
3. Marble Platform
4. Red Step Bridge
5. Imperial Vault of Heaven
6. Echo Wall
7. Echo Stones
8. Round Altar
9. Hall of Abstinence
10. Temple of Heaven Park

1 Hall of Prayer for Good Harvests

Built in 1420, then rebuilt in 1889, this circular tower, with a conical roof of blue tiles and a gold finial, is the most beautiful building in Beijing *(right)*. One of the most striking facts about it is that it was constructed without the use of a single nail.

2 Painted Caisson Ceiling

The circular ceiling of the Hall of Prayer for Good Harvests has a gilded dragon and phoenix at its center *(below)*. The wood for the four central columns was imported from Oregon, as at the time China had no trees tall enough.

3 Marble Platform

The Hall of Prayer for Good Harvests sits atop three tiers of marble that form a circle 300 ft (90 m) in diameter and 20 ft (6 m) high *(above)*. The balusters on the upper tier are decorated with intricate dragon carvings that serve to signify the imperial nature of the structure.

→ *For more on popular Chinese park activities See pp36–7*

4 Red Step Bridge

A raised walkway of marble and stone that runs exactly along the north-south axis of the temple complex, the Red Step Bridge *(left)* connects the Hall of Prayer for Good Harvests with the Round Altar.

5 Imperial Vault of Heaven

A circular hall made of wood and capped by a conical roof, the Imperial Vault *(below)* once held the wooden spirit tablets that were used in the ceremonies that took place on the nearby Round Altar.

6 Echo Wall

The Imperial Vault is enclosed by the circular Echo Wall, which has the same sonic effects found in some European cathedrals, where even a whisper travels round to a listener on the other side.

7 Echo Stones

There are three rectangular stones at the foot of the staircase leading up to the Imperial Vault: stand on the first and clap to hear one echo; stand on the second stone and clap once for two echoes; clap once on the third for three echoes.

8 Round Altar

The altar is formed of marble slabs laid in nine concentric circles with each circle containing a multiple of nine pieces. The center of the altar *(right)* represents the center of the world and it is where the emperor carried out sacrifices.

9 Hall of Abstinence

A red-walled compound surrounded by a moat spanned by decorative bridges, the Hall of Abstinence resembles a mini Forbidden City. This is where the emperor would spend the last 24 hours of his three-day fast prior to partaking in the Temple of Heaven ceremonies.

10 Temple of Heaven Park

Today, locals, inured both to the splendor of the buildings and to the crowds of tourists, use the extensive grounds to practice *tai ji quan (right)*, and other martial arts, and to exercise.

Tian Tan

The Hall of Prayer for Good Harvests, or Qinian Dian, which is the iconic structure at the heart of the complex, is often incorrectly called the Temple of Heaven. There is, in fact, no single temple building and the name, which in Chinese is Tian Tan – a more literal translation of which is Altar of Heaven – refers to the whole complex.

There are also ceremonial sacrificial altars at Zhong Shan, Di Tan, and Ri Tan Parks **See p69, p81 & p87**

⁝⁰⁝10 Tian'an Men Square

Tian'an Men Guangchang (the Square of the Gate of Heavenly Peace) is not one of the world's most attractive public plazas. It also has unfortunate associations with death, in the physical form of Mao's Mausoleum and in the memories of the bloody climax of 1989's pro-democracy demonstrations. But it has witnessed triumphant events too, including the founding of the People's Republic of China, and it remains central to modern life in Beijing, surrounded by important national institutions and filled daily with visitors and kite flyers.

Mao's portrait still hangs from Tian'an Men

🍴 Cafés and restaurants ring the square, but there are better places a short walk south of Qian Men.

🛈 Tian'an Men Square is a heavily symbolic place, so your bags may be inspected.

Tian'an Men Square
- *Map L5*
- *Subway: Tian'an Men West, Tian'an Men East, or Qian Men*
- *National Museum of China: 6511 6400. Open 9am–5pm Tue–Sun (Jul & Aug 8am–6pm)*
- *Mao's Mausoleum: 6513 2277. Open 8am–noon Tue–Sun. Free with valid ID. Handbags, backpacks, cameras, food, and drinks are strictly prohibited*
- *Qian Men: 6522 9384. Open 8:30am–4pm daily. Admission: ¥20*
- *Tian'an Men (Gate of Heavenly Peace): 6524 3322. Open 8:30am–4:30pm daily. Admission: ¥15*

Top 10 Features

1. Tian'an Men
2. National Museum of China
3. Mao's Mausoleum
4. Great Hall of the People
5. Monument to the Heroes
6. Qian Men
7. Arrow Tower
8. National Flag
9. Qian Men Old Railway Station
10. Bicycles

1 Tian'an Men
Mao proclaimed the founding of the People's Republic of China on October 1, 1949 from this massive Ming-dynasty gate *(above)*, where his huge portrait still hangs. The way to the Forbidden City is through here.

2 National Museum of China
This 1959 building on the eastern side of the square *(right)* combines two former museums – the Museum of Chinese History and the Museum of the Revolution. The vast museum has 48 galleries showing Chinese history, art, and archaeology exhibits.

3 Mao's Mausoleum
In an imposing hall at the center of the square *(above)* lies the embalmed body of Mao, who died in 1976. Encased in a crystal casket and draped in a red flag, he is raised from his refrigerated chamber for daily public viewings.

 Come to Tian'an Men Square at sunrise or sunset to watch the flag-raising or flag-lowering ceremony

4 Great Hall of the People

A monolithic structure dominating the western side of the square, the Great Hall is the seat of the Chinese legislature. The vast auditorium and banqueting halls are open for part of every day except when the People's Congress is in session.

5 Monument to the Heroes

Erected in 1958, the granite monument *(left)* is decorated with bas-reliefs of episodes from the nation's revolutionary history and calligraphy from Communist veterans Mao Zedong and Zhou Enlai.

6 Qian Men

The "Front Gate", also known as Zhengyang Men ("Sun facing Gate"), was constructed during the Ming dynasty and was the largest of the nine gates of the inner city wall. It now houses a city history museum.

7 Arrow Tower

With the Qian Men, the Arrow Gate *(above)* formed part of a great double gate. The walls that once flanked the gate were demolished in the 20th century.

8 National Flag

At the northern end of the square is a towering pole, from which flies the Chinese flag; a troop of People's Liberation Army (PLA) soldiers raises the flag each day at dawn and lowers it again at sunset.

9 Qian Men Old Railway Station

The stripy building on the square's southeast corner is a British-built railway station. It now houses shops, an Internet café, a branch of McDonald's, and a theater where performances of Beijing Opera take place.

10 Bicycles

The bicycle remains the quintessentially Chinese way of getting around. While 10 million bikes are registered in Beijing, every day as many as 1,300 new cars are added to the city's congested roads. Smog is a serious problem.

City Walls

It was during the Ming era (1368–1644) that the walls took on their recognizable shape of an outer wall with seven gates, and an inner wall with nine gates. Tragically, almost all was demolished in the 1950s and 1960s, although a small portion still stands south of Beijing Station. The gates are remembered in the names of the subway stations on the Second Ring Road.

For a look at the Tian'an Men area as it used to be, visit the Imperial City Museum See p68

TOP 10 Lama Temple (Yonghegong)

Beijing's most spectacular place of worship is also the most famous Buddhist temple outside of Tibet. It has five main halls, as well as some stunning statuary. The path through the Lama Temple proceeds from south to north – from earth to heaven.

Imperial dragon decoration

💬 There are various snack kiosks inside the Lama Temple, but it is a better idea to bring your own refreshments.

📷 Photography is not allowed within the halls, but you can take pictures of the exteriors and of the courtyards.

12 Yonghe Gong Dajie
• *Map F1*
• *6404 4499*
• *Subway: Yonghe Gong*
• *Open: Apr–Oct 9am–4.30pm daily. Nov–Mar 9am–4pm daily*
• *Admission: ¥25*
• *Audio guides are available for ¥20 (plus ¥200 deposit)*
• *www.yonghegong.cn*

Top 10 Features

1. Monks
2. Drum and Bell Towers
3. Hall of the Heavenly Kings
4. Hall of Eternal Harmony
5. Hall of Eternal Protection
6. Hall of the Wheel of Dharma
7. Hall of Ten Thousand Happinesses
8. Prayer Wheel
9. Incense Burner
10. Lion Statue

1 Monks
At one time there were 1,500 monks at the temple, now there are only 70. Although of the same Yellow Hat sect as the Dalai Lama the monks are required to reject Tibetan independence.

2 Drum and Bell Towers
The temple's Drum and Bell towers are in the first courtyard after passing through the main entrance. The huge bell has been removed from its tower and placed on the ground.

3 Hall of the Heavenly Kings
The first hall has a plump laughing Buddha, Milefo, back-to-back with Wei Tuo, the Guardian of Buddhist Doctrine. They are flanked by the Four Heavenly Kings.

4 Hall of Eternal Harmony
This, the second hall *(left)*, contains three manifestations of Buddha. These represent the past, present, and future, and are flanked by 18 *luohan* – those freed from the cycle of rebirth.

Share your travel recommendations on traveldk.com

5 Hall of Eternal Protection

The third hall contains Buddhas of longevity and medicine. It also has two famous *tangkas*, said to have been embroidered by Emperor Qianlong's mother. Behind the hall is a bronze sculpture of Mount Meru, the center of the Buddhist universe.

6 Hall of the Wheel of Dharma

Hall four has a 20-foot (6-m) high statue of Tsongkhapa, the 14th-century founder of the Yellow Hat sect of Buddhism. Dominant in Tibetan politics for centuries, the sect is led by the Dalai Lama and Panchen Lama.

7 Hall of Ten Thousand Happinesses

The final pavilion *(left)* houses an 80-foot (25-m) high Buddha carved from a single piece of sandalwood. There's a splendid collection of Tibetan Buddhist objects in a room behind the hall.

8 Prayer Wheel

Spinning a prayer wheel *(right)* sends a prayer written on coiled paper to heaven. A little yellow arrow taped to the frame of the wheel reminds worshipers which direction (clockwise) to spin the wheel.

9 Incense Burner

There are incense burners in front of all the many altars throughout the temple. Shops lining the entryway to the complex and in the neighboring streets are piled with bundles of incense sticks for sale for use at the temple.

10 Lion Statue

A large imperial lion *(right)* is a reminder that the complex was originally the residence of the man who would become Qing emperor Yongzheng. On ascending the throne in 1722, and in keeping with tradition, his former home became a temple.

Panchen Lama

While the Dalai Lama, head of the sect to which the Lama Temple belongs, lives in exile, the second head, the Panchen Lama, resides in Beijing. In contrast to the Dalai Lama, the Panchen recognizes Chinese authority. However, the matter of the true identity of the Panchen Lama is a matter of controversy. China supports one candidate, while the Tibetans recognize another – only he vanished in suspicious circumstances in 1995.

→ For more Beijing places of worship **See pp46–7**

17

🔟 Bei Hai Park

An imperial garden for more than a thousand years, Bei Hai was opened to the public in 1925. Filled with artificial hills, pavilions, and temples, it is associated with Kublai Khan, who redesigned it during the Mongol Yuan dynasty. These days, it is a fine place for a leisurely afternoon stroll, and perhaps a bit of boating on the lake.

Lakeside pavilions

Park gate

🍴 Aside from the famous Fangshan Restaurant, there are also small snack kiosks in the park.

🚪 There are four gates to the park: the most convenient is the south gate, close to the northwest corner of the Forbidden City; the north gate exits across the road from Hou Hai, where there are good eating and drinking options.

1 Wenjin Jie, Xicheng
• Map K1
• 6403 3225
• Subway: Tian'an Men West
• Buses: 5, 101, 103, 107, 109, 111, and others
• Open: Apr–Oct 6am–10pm daily. Nov–Mar 6:30am–9pm. All buildings close at 5pm Apr–Oct, 4pm Nov–Mar
• Admission: Apr–Oct ¥10. Nov–Mar ¥5
• www.beihaipark.com.cn

Top 10 Features

1. Round City
2. Jade Island
3. White Dagoba
4. Yongan Temple
5. Fangshan Restaurant
6. Pavilion of Calligraphy
7. The Place of Serenity
8. Xiao Xitian Temple
9. Nine Dragon Screen
10. Zhong Nan Hai

Round City
Bei Hai was the site of Beijing's earliest imperial palace, although nothing remains other than a small pavilion on a site known as the Round City, and a large jade wine vessel said to have belonged to Kublai Khan.

Jade Island
Accessed by bridge from the south gate or by boat from the north gate, Bei Hai's willow-lined island *(right)* was created from the earth excavated to form the lake.

White Dagoba
Topping Jade Island, the 118-ft (36-m) high White Dagoba is a Tibetan-style stupa built to honor the visit of the fifth Dalai Lama in 1651. It has been rebuilt twice since.

Yongan Temple
Beneath the Dagoba, the temple comprises a series of ascending halls, including the Hall of the Wheel of Law with its central effigy of the Buddha Sakyamuni.

Fangshan Restaurant
Founded in 1926 by chefs of the imperial household, the restaurant *(left)* bases its menus on court cuisine. Standards have slipped but the lakeside setting still has great appeal.

6 Pavilion of Calligraphy

A crescent-shaped hall on Jade Island contains nearly 500 stone tablets engraved with the work of famous Chinese calligraphers. If the exhibits are less than enthralling the walkways that lead to the pavilion are enchanting.

7 The Place of Serenity

In the northwest corner of the park is this beautiful garden *(left)*, created in the mid-18th century by the Qianlong emperor, with rockeries, pavilions, and ornate bridges over goldfish-filled pools.

8 Xiao Xitian Temple

Near the Place of Serenity is a trio of small temple buildings – the Pavilion of 10,000 Buddhas, the Glazed Pavilion, which is covered with green and yellow ceramic Buddhas, and the Xiao Xitian (Small Western Sky) Temple filled with fearsome-looking idols *(above)*.

9 Nine Dragon Screen

Bei Hai's most striking sight is an 89-ft (27-m) long, free-standing wall made of colorful glazed ceramic tiles and depicting nine intertwined dragons *(below)*. The Chinese dragon is a beneficent beast offering protection and good luck. The wall was designed to obstruct the passage of evil spirits, who are only able to travel in straight lines.

10 Zhong Nan Hai

Bei Hai means North Lake; the Middle (Zhong) and South (Nan) Lakes are part of an area occupied by China's political leaders and are off-limits to all except government officials. Zhong Nan Hai is regarded as the new Forbidden City.

Park play

Beijing's parks double as recreation centers, particularly for the city's elderly citizens. As soon as the parks open in the morning they gather to perform communal *tai ji quan* (tai chi) exercises. Many then spend the rest of the day in the park playing cards, dominos or mahjong, engaging in *yang ge* (fan dancing) or ballroom dancing, or simply reading the newspaper and talking with friends.

10 Hou Hai

The area around the joined lakes of Qian Hai and Hou Hai has traditionally been home to nobles and wealthy merchants. Several grand homes survive, hidden in the labyrinthine old lanes known as hutongs. *This is a rare quarter of Beijing where the 21st century is kept at bay, and these back alleys represent one of the most satisfying parts of the city to explore on foot – or by rickshaw.*

Al fresco dining at Qian Hai

Gaudy lamp shades for sale on Yandai Xie Jie

⊙ The Hou Hai area has several excellent restaurants and bars, *see pp82–3.*

🟢 Visit Hou Hai by day to explore the *hutongs* and historic residences, but do come back by night to dine and see the lake glimmering with the flotilla of tea-candles that are floated out on the water each evening.

Map D2 • Subway: Gulou Dajie, Jishuitan
• Mansion of Prince Gong: 8328 8149. Open: 8:30am–4:30pm daily. Admission: ¥40 or ¥70 with tour guide, tea, and snack tasting, and traditional opera performance (call ahead for times)
• Former Residence of Guo Moruo: 6612 5984. Open 9am–4.30pm Tue–Sun. Closed Dec 25 until 5th day of Chinese New Year. Admission: ¥20
• Song Qingling's Residence: 6404 4205. Open 9am–5:30pm (Nov–Mar to 4:30pm) Tue–Sun. Admission: ¥20

Top 10 Features

1 Lotus Lane
2 Boating and skating
3 Silver Ingot Bridge
4 Hutongs
5 Mansion of Prince Gong
6 Former Residence of Guo Moruo
7 Rickshaw tours
8 Song Qingling's Residence
9 Yandai Xie Jie
10 Drum and Bell Towers

1 Lotus Lane

This is the tourist-friendly name attached to Hou Hai's main lakeside parade of restaurants, bars, and cafés. Many of these establishments feature attractive waterfront terraces.

2 Boating and skating

In summer the lakes are filled with small pedal boats, rented by the hour. By mid-December, they are frozen over *(above)* and a large area is corraled off for public ice-skating.

3 Silver Ingot Bridge

The narrow channel that connects Hou Hai's two lakes is spanned by the pretty, arched Silver Ingot Bridge *(right)*, which dates from the time of the Yuan dynasty (1279–1368).

4 Hutongs

The lakes lie at the heart of a sprawling old Beijing district, characterized by the traditional alleyways known as *hutongs*. These alleyways are lined for the most part by the blank outer walls of *siheyuan*, which are inward-looking houses that are arranged around a central courtyard. Each *siheyuan* houses several families.

Mansion of Prince Gong 5

Built for a Manchu official but seized by the imperial household, the former residence of Prince Gong is the best preserved historic mansion in Beijing. The garden is a pattern of corridors and pavilions, dotted with pools and gates *(right)*.

6 Former Residence of Guo Moruo

Beijing has countless "former residences of," mostly connected with Party favorites. Moruo was an author and influential figure in the rise of communism in China. His house offers the opportunity to see inside a *hutong* home.

7 Rickshaw tours

One way of seeing the *hutongs* is from a rickshaw. Prices and length of the tour are negotiable, but expect to pay around ¥180 per person for a two-hour jaunt with stop-offs at several place of interest.

8 Song Qingling's Residence

Song Qingling was the wife of the revolutionary leader Sun Yat Sen. Her former living quarters are now a small museum (note the pistol that Sun Yat Sen gave his wife as a wedding present). The gardens surrounding the house are beautiful.

10 Drum and Bell Towers

Just north of the eastern end of Yandai Xie Jie these two imposing towers *(above)* once marked the northern-most limits of the city. You can ascend the towers for views of Hou Hai and beyond.

9 Yandai Xie Jie

One of the loveliest streets in Beijing is lined with historic buildings *(main pic)*, most of which have been converted into small boutiques and bars, including a temple that is now a café.

Siheyuan

Traditional Beijing homes are arranged around a central courtyard. The main dwelling is on the north, with lesser halls on the other three sides. Originally homes of the well-to-do, over time many *siheyuan* were occupied by poorer families, who squeezed several households into the space formerly occupied by one. Modernization has destroyed many of these dwellings, but there is a movement to preserve those that have survived. A few have been converted into hotels *(see p116)*.

Beijing's Top 10

→ *For more on Hou Hai and around* See pp78–83

Summer Palace (Yiheyuan)

A sprawling landscaped park on the edge of the city, this seasonal imperial retreat from the stifling confines of the Forbidden City was the favored haunt of Empress Cixi. She had it rebuilt twice: once after its destruction by French and English troops in 1860, and again in 1902, after it was plundered during the Boxer Rebellion.

Sea of Wisdom temple

Painted ceiling in the Long Corridor

🍴 There are several small snack kiosks in the park grounds.

⚠ Avoid visiting on days with poor visibility when you risk missing the superb views across the lake that are one of the highlights of a visit to the Summer Palace.

6 miles (10 km) NW of central Beijing
• 6288 1144
• Subway: Bagou, then bus 394
• Open: Apr–Oct 6:30am–6pm (park), 8:30am–5pm (sights) daily. Nov–Mar 7am–5pm (park), 9am–4pm (sights) daily. Last admission 2 hrs before closing
• Admission: ¥60 all inclusive, ¥30 park only
• Audio guides are available for ¥40 (plus ¥200 deposit)
• www.summerpalace-china.com

Top 10 Features

1. Hall of Happiness and Longevity
2. Garden of Virtue and Harmony
3. Long Corridor
4. Longevity Hill
5. Tower of the Fragrance of the Buddha
6. Temple of the Sea of Wisdom
7. Marble Boat
8. Suzhou Street
9. South Lake Island
10. Seventeen-arch Bridge

1 Hall of Happiness and Longevity

This impressive hall was the residence of the Empress Cixi. It has supposedly been left just as it was at the time of her death in 1908, complete with its Qing dynasty-era furniture.

2 Garden of Virtue and Harmony

This pretty complex of roofed corridors, small pavilions, rock gardens and pools also includes Cixi's private three-story theater *(left)*. The buildings now contain Qing-era artifacts, from vehicles to costumes and glassware.

3 Long Corridor

From the Garden of Virtue and Harmony the aptly named Long Corridor zigzags along the shore of the lake, interrupted along its length by four pavilions. The ceilings and beams of this corridor are decorated with over 14,000 scenic paintings.

It is possible to get out to the Summer Palace by boat on the old canal system See p106

Longevity Hill
At around the halfway point of the Long Corridor a series of buildings ascends the slopes of artificially created Longevity Hill *(below)*. The start of the sequence is marked at the lakeside by a very fine decorative gate, or *pailou*.

Tower of the Fragrance of the Buddha
Toward the peak of Longevity Hill rises this prominent octagonal tower. The stiff climb is rewarded with views from the balcony over the yellow roofs of the halls and pavilions to the lake below.

Kunmi Lake

Temple of the Sea of Wisdom
North of the Fragrance of the Buddha tower is a green- and yellow-tiled temple decorated with glazed Buddhist effigies, many of which have sadly been vandalized.

Marble Boat
Cixi paid for this extravagant folly *(above)* with funds meant for the modernization of the Imperial Navy. The superstructure of the boat is made of wood painted white to look like marble. Boat trips to South Lake Island depart from a neighboring jetty.

Suzhou Street
At the foot of Longevity Hill on its north side is Suzhou Street, a shopping street built for the amusement of the Qianlong emperor, his concubines and eunuchs, who would play at being shoppers, shopkeepers, and pickpockets.

South Lake Island
Crowning this small island on the south side of Kunming Lake is the Dragon King Temple (Longwang Miao), which is dedicated to the god of rivers, seas, and rain.

Seventeen-arch Bridge
South Lake Island is connected to the eastern shore by an elegant bridge *(above)* with a marble lion crowning each of the 544 balusters along its length, all supposedly individual. A large bronze ox, dating back to 1755 but looking entirely modern, reposes on the eastern shore.

Beijing's Top 10

Empress Cixi

Cixi is remembered as one of China's most powerful women. Having borne one emperor's son as an imperial concubine, she became the power behind the throne to two more: her son and her nephew. When she blocked state reforms and lent support to the xenophobic Boxers in their rebellion, she unwittingly paved the way for the end of the imperial era.

For more parks and gardens See p37

798 Art District

Since the first artists set up in Da Shan Zi's newly vacated 798 factory in 2001, the East German-built industrial compound has become a world-famous center of contemporary Chinese art. Alongside the studios and galleries, there are also chic cafés, bars, and restaurants, not to mention a growing number of designer shops and showrooms. The area is popular with tourists, who arrive by the coach-load.

798 factory

Graffiti-daubed wall in the factory compound

ℹ The Ullens Center for Contemporary Art provides free maps of the entire 798 area. Most galleries are open from around 11am to 7pm, closed on Mondays.

4 Jiu Xian Qiao Lu, Chaoyang district, northeast of the Metro Park Lido complex
• Bus: 401, 402, 405, 445, 909, 955, 973, 988, 991. To Caochangdi: Bus 418 from Dongzhimen
• 798 Space: 5978 9180. Open: 10:30am–7:30pm daily.
www.798space.com
• UCCA: 5780 0200. Open: 10am–7pm Tue–Sun. Admission: ¥15 (free on Thu).
www.ucca.org.cn
• Galleria Continua: 5979 9505. Open: 11am–6pm Tue–Sun.
www.galleriacontinua.com
• Iberia Center for Contemporary Art: 5978 9530. Open: 10am–6pm Tue–Sun.
www.iberiart.org

Top 10 Features

1. 798 Space
2. Maoist graffiti
3. AT Café
4. UCCA
5. White Space
6. Timezone 8
7. Galleria Continua
8. Iberia Center for Contemporary Art
9. Caochangdi
10. 798 Photo Gallery

1 798 Space
The first gallery to open in Da Shan Zi, 798 Space *(above)* remains at the heart of the district. It is worth visiting for the spectacle of the cavernous main hall with its curious multiple-arched roof.

2 Maoist graffiti
When many of the abandoned factory spaces were being converted for use as galleries, the artists instructed the decorators to leave untouched the giant Maoist slogans that had been lettered on the walls by the former workers – as at 798 Space *(left)*. "Mao Zedong is the red star in our hearts," reads one.

3 AT Café
A fashionable café whose notable feature is a bare-brick dividing wall punctured by massive holes, AT *(left)* serves as the unofficial canteen for the artists and gallery staff who work in the area.

For arts festivals and fairs See p35

4 UCCA

Founded by Belgian collectors Guy and Miriam Ullens, the Ullens Center for Contemporary Art (UCCA) is the largest single venue in the 798 area. Among the many artists showing here is Fang Lijun *(below)*. UCCA has an auditorium for lectures and films, a store, and a restaurant.

5 White Space

Foreign art dealers are already present in numbers in 798. The striking White Space was one of the first such galleries, a branch of the Berlin-based Alexander Ochs Gallery.

6 Timezone 8

Established in 2001 by Texan Robert Bernell, Timezone 8 *(below)*, which occupies a former factory canteen, is Beijing's best art book-shop. It also incorporates a gallery that specializes in photographic art.

7 Galleria Continua

Beijing's outpost of Italy's Galleria Continua is located in a former munitions factory. This gallery, which aims to stimulate cultural exchanges, hosts shows by renowned international artists such as Chen Zhen, Antony Gormley, Daniel Buren, and Anish Kapoor.

8 Iberia Center for Contemporary Art

The second major European-funded space in Da Shan Zi, Iberia *(left)* is proof of 798's leap from the local to the international scene. In addition to an exhibition area, Iberia has a public education center, a publishing house, and a media archive.

10 798 Photo Gallery

In addition to often excellent and regularly changing exhibitions of work by both Chinese and foreign photographers, the gallery also has a couple of mezzanine levels where a selection of photographic prints for sale are displayed.

9 Caochangdi

While 798 looks like a retail outlet, Caochangdi, set in a more bucolic location farther out of the city, has emerged as a truly cutting-edge art district. It is the home of Ai Weiwei, China's influential Bird's Nest architect *(see p40)*, plus Pekin Fine Arts, Egg Gallery, and Platform China.

Brave new worlds

1985 marks the arrival of the avant garde in Chinese art, with controversial student graduation shows igniting intense debate in artistic circles. The following year, a New York gallery introduced the new Chinese art to an international audience. Today, China's art market is the third largest in the world.

For more Beijing galleries to visit **See p49**

TOP 10 Ming Tombs

The resting place for 13 of the 16 Ming-dynasty (1368–1644) emperors, this is China's finest example of imperial funerary architecture. The site was selected because of its auspicious feng shui alignment; a ridge of mountains to the north cradles the tombs on three sides, protecting the dead from the evil spirits carried on the north wind. The tombs are spread over 15 square miles (40 sq km). Three (Chang Ling, Ding Ling, and Zhao Ling) have been restored and are always busy. Unrestored, the rest are open but quiet.

The Great Palace Gate, leading to the Spirit Way

🍴 There are snack kiosks at the site.

🚌 The Ming Tombs are most conveniently seen as part of a trip to the Great Wall at Badaling. Many hotels will arrange tours. The government-operated Tour Bus 2 leaves regularly for the tombs and the Great Wall from just east of Qian Men on Tian'an Men Square every day from 6:30am onwards; the fare is ¥50 per person.

30 miles (45 km) NW of Beijing
• 6076 1422
• Bus 345 to Changping Dongguan, then bus 314 to the tombs
• Open: Apr–Oct 8am–5pm (Ding Ling to 5:30pm) daily. Nov–Mar 8:30am–4:30pm (Ding Ling to 5pm)
• Admission: Spirit Way ¥30. Chang Ling ¥45 (¥30 off-peak). Ding Ling ¥65 (¥45 off-peak). Zhao Ling ¥30 (¥20 off-peak)
• www.mingtombs.com

Top 10 Features

1. Memorial Arch
2. Stele Pavilion
3. Spirit Way
4. Chang Ling Tomb
5. Hall of Eminent Favor
6. Ding Ling Treasures
7. Spirit Tower
8. Ding Ling Tomb
9. Ding Ling Burial Chamber
10. Zhao Ling Tomb

Memorial Arch
Marking the entrance to the site is a magnificent five-arched gate (below), built of white marble, and erected in 1540. At 40 ft (12 m) high and more than 92 ft (28 m) wide, it is the largest of its kind in China, and boasts beautiful bas-relief carvings.

Spirit Way
Part of the 4-mile (7-km) approach to the tombs, the Spirit Way (above) is lined with 18 pairs of giant guardians – stone statues of court officials, imperial warriors, animals, and mythical Chinese beasts.

Stele Pavilion
After the Memorial Arch the road passes through the Great Palace Gate and the tunnel-like arch of the Stele Pavilion. Here the largest stele in China projects from the shell of a giant *bixi* (dragon-tortoise) and bears the names of the emperors buried at the site.

Chang Ling Tomb
The resting place of the Yongle emperor (left), the builder of the Forbidden City and Temple of Heaven, is the oldest and grandest tomb. It has been well restored, but the chamber where Yongle, his wife, and 16 concubines are buried has never been excavated.

 Share your travel recommendations on traveldk.com

5 Hall of Eminent Favor

One of China's most impressive surviving Ming buildings, this double-eaved sacrificial hall is the centerpiece of the Chang Ling tomb complex. It stands on a triple-tiered marble terrace and 32 gigantic cedar columns *(left)* support the roof.

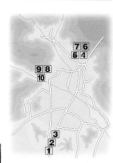

6 Ding Ling Treasures

In addition to an impressive statue of the Yongle emperor, the Hall of Eminent Favor also contains artifacts from the Wanli emperor's tomb (the Ding Ling). These include a crown of golden wire topped by two dragons *(above)*.

8 Ding Ling Tomb

This is the tomb of the longest-reigning Ming ruler, the emperor Wanli (1573–1620). His profligate rule began the downfall of the dynasty. Building his tomb involved 30,000 workers and took six years to complete.

7 Spirit Tower

Rising up from the third courtyard of the Chang Ling complex, the tower marks the entrance to the burial chamber. This takes the form of an earthen tumulus girdled by a wall half a mile (1 km) in circumference.

9 Ding Ling Burial Chamber

This is the only burial chamber to be excavated and opened to the public. Visitors descend to a central throne room and a rear annex with three red-lacquer coffins *(left)*, belonging to Wanli and his two wives.

10 Zhao Ling Tomb

The resting place of the 13th Ming emperor, Longqing (1537–72), who gained the throne at the age of 30 and died six years later. It has an attractive triple-bridge over a stream.

The Ming dynasty

The 276-year Ming ("brilliant") dynasty rule was one of the longest and most stable periods in Chinese history. The founder of the Ming rose from humble beginnings via military successes to become emperor. He was succeeded by his grandson, who, in turn was succeeded by his son, who proclaimed himself emperor Yongle ("Eternal Joy"). It was Yongle who moved the capital from Nanjing to Beijing where he created a new city.

 For more daytrips out of Beijing **See pp98–101**

Great Wall of China

The Great Wall snakes through the countryside over deserts, hills, and plains for several thousand miles. At its closest point it is less than 40 miles (60 km) from Beijing. The wall was created following the unification of China under Qin Shi Huangdi (221–210 BC). Despite impressive battlements, it ultimately proved ineffective; it was breached in the 13th century by the Mongols and again, in the 17th century, by the Manchus. Today, only select sections of its crumbling remains have been fully restored, with four main sites accessible from Beijing: Badaling, Mutianyu, Huanghua Cheng, and Simatai.

Souvenir stall at Badaling

🕐 The area is extremely hot in summer (bring sun cream and lots of water) and bitterly cold in winter.

🍴 There are snack kiosks at each of the main four sites, but it's better to bring your own food.

Badaling 44 miles (70 km) NW of Beijing • 6912 2222 • Bus 919 from Desheng Men • Open 7am–6pm daily • ¥40

Mutianyu 56 miles (90 km) N of Beijing • 6162 6505 • Bus 916 from Dong Zhi Men bus station; change at Huairou • Open 7am–6pm daily • ¥40

Huanghua Cheng 37 miles (60 km) N of Beijing • 6165 1044 • Open 8am–5pm Mon–Fri, 7:30am–5:30pm Sat & Sun • ¥25

Simatai 68 miles (110 km) NE of Beijing • 6903 1051 • Bus 980 from Dong Zhi Men bus station, then taxi • Currently closed; due to reopen in 2013

Top 10 Features

1. Badaling
2. Great Wall Museum
3. Juyong Guan
4. Commune by the Great Wall
5. Mutianyu
6. Huanghua Cheng
7. Simatai
8. Jingshanling
9. Gubeikou
10. Shanhaiguan

Badaling
The restored Ming fortification at Badaling (below) is the closest section of the wall to Beijing. Its accessibility means it is perpetually busy. However, it is possible to escape the crowds by walking along the wall; and the views are spectacular.

Great Wall Museum
Housed in an imitation Qing dynasty building at Badaling, the museum presents the history of the region from neolithic times, as well as detailing the construction of the wall. Admission is covered in the cost of your wall ticket.

Juyong Guan
This pass is on the way to Badaling. With unscalable mountains on either side it is easy to see why the spot was chosen for defence. Early cannons remain on the ramparts (below). Also worth seeing are Buddhist carvings on a stone platform, or "cloud terrace," in the middle of the pass.

Commune by the Great Wall

Within sight of the wall at Badaling, the Commune *(right)* consists of 12 contemporary villas, each designed by a different, celebrated Asian architect. The complex operates as a hotel *(see p113)*, but non-guests can drop by the restaurant for lunch, or take an architecture tour.

Mutianyu

Located in a dramatic hilly setting, and with a series of watchtowers along its restored length, the wall here dates from 1368. Village buildings have been converted into holiday homes and restaurants.

Huanghua Cheng

On the same stretch of wall as Mutianyu, Huanghua Cheng *(below)* is an exhilarating section of Ming fortifications that is far less developed than most other parts. The great barrier is split into two by a large reservoir. The crumbling masonry can be uneven and fairly treacherous, so you need to take care.

Gubeikou

Lying farther west of Jingshanling, Gubeikou is a heavily fortified pass from where you can begin a 15-mile (25-km) walk to Simatai. It is, if you are really fit, possible to do it in one day.

Shanhaiguan

This is where the wall ends (or begins), at the sea. East of town, the "First Pass Under Heaven" is a formidable section of wall attached to a gatehouse. It lies some 218 miles (350 km) east of Beijing but it does make for a worthwhile overnight trip.

Simatai

The wall at Simatai *(above)* has long been a favorite for adventurers because of its raw, untouched aspect. However, this section is undergoing redevelopment and major portions may be closed or fenced off until fall 2013.

Jingshanling

The starting point for a 6-mile (10-km) trek to Simatai, which because of the steep and stony trail usually takes around four hours. The views as the wall winds over sharp peak after sharp peak are fantastic, but you have to work for them.

Visiting the wall

Most hotels are able to organize a trip to the wall, usually combined with a visit to the Ming Tombs *(see pp26–7)*. Try to find out whether there are any unwanted diversions to cloisonné workshops, jade factories, or Chinese medicine clinics. Small groups can have a more personalized visit, and see the more remote parts of the wall, by hiring a taxi for the day from Beijing. Hiking clubs in Beijing offer day trips to lesser-known parts of the wall.

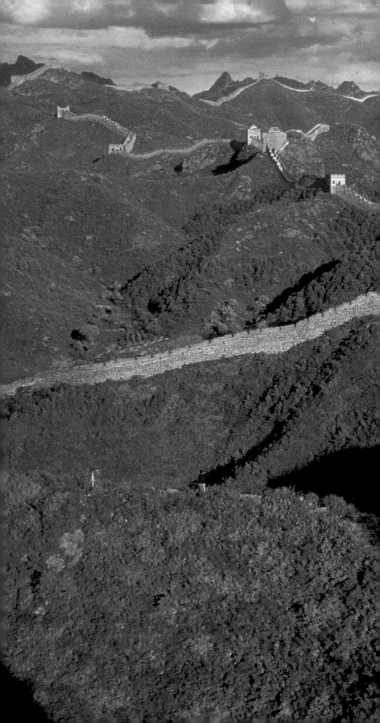

Left **Mongol horsemen** Center **Empress Cixi** Right **Red Army tank**

Moments in History

1 500,000 BC: Peking Man hunts and gathers

Unearthed in the 1920s from a cave at Zhoukoudian, 30 miles (45 km) SW of Beijing, 40-odd fossilized bones and primitive implements were identified as the prehistoric remains of Peking Man *(Homo erectus Pekinensis)*, who lived in the vicinity over 500,000 years ago.

2 1215: Genghis Khan sacks Zhongdu

The future Beijing was developed as an auxiliary capital under the Liao (907–1125) and Jin dynasties (1115–1234), at which time it was known as Zhongdu. In 1215 it was invaded and razed by a Mongol army led by the fearsome Genghis Khan.

3 Late 13th century: Marco Polo visits

Under the first emperor of the Mongol Yuan dynasty, Kublai Khan (r. 1260–1294), the city became known as Khanbalik, and was one of twin capitals – the other was Yuanshangdu, or Xanadu – of the largest empire ever known. The Italian traveler Marco Polo was dazzled by the imperial palace: "The building is altogether so vast and beautiful, that no man on earth could design anything superior to it."

4 1403–25: Construction of the Forbidden City

The Ming emperor Yongle (r. 1403–24) destroyed the palaces of his Mongol predecessors in order to rebuild the city, which he renamed Beijing (Northern Capital). He is credited with laying the foundations for the city as it is today, and the Forbidden City and Temple of Heaven began to take shape during his reign.

"Last Emperor" Pu Yi

5 1900: Boxer Rebellion

Western powers, frustrated by the reluctance of the Chinese to open up to foreign trade, put the imperial court under pressure, eventually going to war to protect their trade in opium. In 1900, championed by the Empress Cixi, a band of rebels from north China known as the Boxers attacked Beijing's Foreign Legation Quarter. A joint eight-nation army had to be sent to lift the siege.

6 1912: The End of Empire

The last emperor, Pu Yi, ascended the throne at the age of three. Four years later, in February 1912, his brief reign was brought to a premature end when he was forced to abdicate by general Yuan Shikai's new National Assembly.

7 1949: Founding of the People's Republic of China

On January 31, 1949, Communist forces led by Mao Zedong seized Beijing. On October 1, Mao proclaimed the foundation of the People's Republic of China from the gallery of the Tian'an Men.

8 1965: Launch of the Cultural Revolution

Having socialized industry and agriculture, Mao called on the masses to transform society itself. All distinctions between manual and intellectual work were to be abolished and the class system was to be eradicated. The revolution reached its violent peak in 1967, with the Red Guards spreading fear and havoc.

9 1976: The death of Mao

On September 9, 1976 Mao died. The destructive policies of the Cultural Revolution were abandoned. Mao's long-time opponent Deng Xiaoping emerged as leader, implementing reforms that encouraged greater economic freedom.

10 2008: Beijing hosts the Olympics

In 2008, Beijing hosted the Olympic Games. The city revamped its infrastructures, and some of the most striking and innovative buildings were created to house the various competitions *(see pp40–41)*.

Opening ceremony of the 2008 Olympics

Top 10 Chinese Inventions

1 Porcelain
The Chinese invented porcelain a thousand years before Europe caught on – and kept production methods secret to protect their competitive advantage.

2 Printing
In the 11th century, the Chinese carved individual characters on pieces of clay, inventing movable block type.

3 Paper money
Developed by Chinese merchants as certificates of exchange. Lighter than coins, bills were soon adopted by the government.

4 Gunpowder
Stumbled on by Daoist alchemists seeking the elixir of life.

5 Seismometer
A ball fell from one of four dragon's mouths to indicate the direction of the quake.

6 Abacus
Invented during the Yuan dynasty and still in use throughout China today.

7 Magnetic compass
Developed from an instrument used for *feng shui* and geomancy, it helped the Chinese explore the world.

8 Paper
A prototype paper was made from mulberry bark, although bamboo, hemp, linen, and silk were also used to write on.

9 Crossbow
Better range, accuracy, and penetration than the standard bow.

10 Decimal system
Developed alongside the writing system and led to mathematical advances.

The Science and Technology Museum includes an exhibition of Chinese inventions **See p96**

Left **Mooncake** Center **Lantern Festival** Right **Dragon Boat Festival**

Festivals and Events

1 Chinese New Year

Also known as Spring Festival, Beijing's favorite holiday is celebrated with a cacophony of fireworks, let off night and day across the city. There are also temple fairs with stilt-walkers, acrobats, and fortune-tellers. Everyone who can heads for their family home, where gifts are exchanged and children are kept quiet with red envelopes stuffed with cash so adults can watch the annual Spring Festival Gala on national television. ◈ *Three days from the first day of the first moon, usually late Jan or early Feb*

2 Lantern Festival

Coinciding with a full moon, this festival marks the end of the 15-day Spring Festival celebrations. Lanterns bearing auspicious characters or in the shape of animals are hung everywhere. It is also a time for eating the sticky rice balls known as *yuanxiao*. ◈ *The 15th day of the lunar calendar (end of Feb)*

Guardian hung on doors to welcome Chinese New Year

3 Tomb-Sweeping Festival

Also known as Qing Ming, this festival is also a public holiday. Chinese families visit their ancestors' graves to tidy them up, make offerings of snacks and alcohol, and burn incense and paper money. ◈ *Apr 5, but Apr 4 in leap years*

4 International Labor Day

A reminder that China is still a Communist nation, Labor Day is celebrated with a three-day holiday, which marks the start of the domestic travel season. Shops, offices, and other businesses close for the entire holiday, and often for a whole week. Don't plan on doing any out-of-town travel during this time. ◈ *May 1*

5 Dragon Boat Festival (Duanwu Jie)

Drums thunder and paddles churn up the water as dragon-headed craft compete for top honors. The festival remembers the honest official, Qu Yuan, who, the story goes, drowned himself 2,500 years ago after banishment from the court of the Duke of Chu. Shocked citizens threw rice cakes into the water to distract the fish from nibbling on his body, hence the wholesale consumption of these delicacies on this date every year. ◈ *The 5th day of the 5th lunar month (early Jun)*

6 Mid-Autumn Festival

Also known as the Harvest or Moon Festival, this is traditionally a time for family reunions and for giving boxes of sweet and savory mooncakes *(yuebing)*. ◈ *The 15th day of the 8th lunar month (usually Sep)*

Cricket-fighting

7 Cricket season in Beijing has nothing to do with the genteel English game. The Chinese version involves ruthless antennae-on-antennae action as cricket-fanciers goad their insects into battle in the plastic bowls that serve as gladiatorial arenas. Once the favorite sport of emperors, it now takes place in backstreets all over town. ⊗ *Mid-Sep to the end of Oct*

National Day

8 Marking the anniversary of Mao's 1949 speech in which he declared the foundation of the People's Republic. Crowds turn out to watch massed parades of high-kicking soldiers, and a jam-packed Tian'an Men Square is colored red by a sea of hand-held, waving flags. ⊗ *Oct 1*

Christmas Day

9 Not a traditional Chinese holiday but the festivities have been adopted via Hong Kong, which means that there is a stress on the commercial aspect. High-street stores are bedecked with *Shengdan Laoren*, the Chinese version of Father Christmas. ⊗ *Dec 25*

New Year's Day

10 Although overshadowed by Chinese New Year, which takes place soon after, Western New Year is still a public holiday throughout China. ⊗ *Jan 1*

National Day parade

Top 10 Annual Cultural Events

1 Chaoyang Festival
Street theater, live music, circus, and dance. ⊗ *Chaoyang Park • Late Jan, early Feb*

2 Temple Fairs
Colorful street fairs outside the city's large temples during Chinese New Year. ⊗ *Jan/Feb*

3 Jue
Major independent arts and music festival showcasing modern Chinese culture. ⊗ *Various venues • Mar*

4 The Bookworm International Literary Festival
A celebration of literature that includes talks by authors from around the world. ⊗ *The Bookworm (see p61) • Mar*

5 Beijing International Film Festival
The nation's largest film festival screens new movies from China, Asia, and the rest of the world. ⊗ *Various venues • Apr*

6 Beijing International Theater Festival
A month of musicals, operas, puppet shows, and dramas. ⊗ *Various venues • May*

7 Midi Music Festival
Home-grown punk, metal, rock, and dance. Venues and dates change. ⊗ *May*

8 Art Beijing
Contemporary art fair with exhibitors from around the globe. ⊗ *National Agricultural Exhibition Center • May*

9 Beijing Biennale
Chinese and international artists showcase their work. ⊗ *National Art Museum • Odd years, late Sep–late Oct*

10 Beijing International Music Festival
Month-long extravaganza of soloists and orchestras. ⊗ *Various venues • Oct*

Left **Outdoor drummers** Center **Playing table tennis** Right **Kite flying**

Outdoor Activities

1 Kite flying
A major hobby among gents of all ages, especially popular on public holidays when the skies above the city's parks and squares are crowded with fluttering birds, dragons, lions, and laughing Buddhas.

2 Mahjong
Like gin rummy it's all about collecting sets or runs to score points, only mahjong uses tiles, not playing cards. A visit to any Beijing park will invariably be soundtracked by the rat-a-tat of slammed pieces.

3 Street dancing
Ballroom dancing is hugely popular with the elderly, but in Beijing it doesn't take place in ballrooms but out on the street. On warm evenings, car parks and sidewalks are filled with dancers congregated around a boombox. At the Workers' Stadium you can get up to four different groups on the forecourt in front of the north gate – choose your style: waltz, polka, foxtrot, or gavotte.

4 Jianzi
Western kids play it with a football, passing the ball around with head, knees, and feet, the idea being not to let it touch the ground; the Chinese have their own version playing with what resembles a large plastic shuttlecock. It's called *jianzi* and it is something of a national obsession, played by young and old alike, male and female.

5 Tai chi
Looking to improve the flow of *qi* (life force) through their bodies, early each morning crowds of mostly elderly people gather in Beijing's parks to indulge in mass movements of *tai chi*, or *tai ji quan* as it's better known in China. Although the discipline has its origins in martial arts, for most folks it's more about making sure that the joints don't seize up.

Water calligraphy

6 Yang Ge
Dancing accessorized with brightly-colored, silk fans (an art known as *yang ge*) is popular with middle-aged ladies. It incorporates stylized movements derived from folk dancing.

Ballroom dancing Beijing style

Singing opera down at the park

Table tennis
7 More than just a game, table tennis, or ping pong, is the national pastime. It is the most widely practised sport by people of all ages. It is affordable to all and played in parks and on squares, with bricks often standing in for a missing net.

Water calligraphy
8 Using a mop-like brush and a bowl of plain water, characters are painted on the sidewalk. Once dry, the characters disappear. It is supposed to exercise the mind and body. Tossing coins into the bowl will not be appreciated.

Opera singing
9 The Chinese are rarely inhibited by self-consciousness and behave in public as they would at home. Hence, parks are for singing. They gather in groups, taking it in turns to perform for each other; favored places for this are on the north shore of the lake at Bei Hai and in the Temple of Heaven park.

Chinese chess
10 Walk along any Beijing alley, and you'll likely pass at least one group of old men playing Chinese chess, with bystanders usually far outnumbering the players. Chinese chess is played with flat round pieces that are placed on the intersections of lines on an uncheckered board.

Top 10 Parks

1 Bei Hai Park
Classic ornamental gardens with a large lake for boating (see pp18–19).

2 Chaoyang Park
The largest afforested park in Beijing, with well-maintained flower and grass areas. Subway: Liangmaqiao

3 Di Tan Park
Large green spaces and cypress trees, and the striking Temple of Earth (see p81).

4 Xiang Shan Park
An hour's drive northwest of the center but worth it for thickly wooded slopes dotted with pavilions (see p95).

5 Olympic Green
A 1,680-acre (680-hectare) green space, Beijing's largest park is home to three Olympic venues (see pp40–41). Subway: Forest Park

6 Jing Shan Park
A hilly park with a pavilion providing views of the roofscape of the Forbidden City to the south (see p68).

7 Long Tan Park
Lots of lakes, a kids' amusement park, and an enchanting water-screen show. Map G6 • Subway: Tian Tan Dong Men

8 Ri Tan Park
One of Beijing's oldest parks, featuring an altar for imperial sacrifice (see p85).

9 Temple of Heaven Park
This park houses several historic structures and a vast expanse of well-tended gardens, including a rose garden (see pp12–13).

10 Zhong Shan Park
Just outside the walls of the Forbidden City, Zhong Shan offers a respite from the crowds (see p69).

For activities for children **See pp52–3**

Left **Beijing Opera cast** Right **Acrobats**

Beijing Opera

Colors
The colors of the performers' painted faces symbolize the individual characters' qualities. Red, for example, represents loyalty and courage. Purple stands for solemnity and a sense of justice, green for bravery and irascibility.

Painted face

Acrobatics
Beijing Opera is a form of "total theater" with singing, speech, mime, and acrobatics that combine graceful gymnastics and movements from the martial arts. Training is notoriously hard. Costumes are designed to make the jumps seem more spectacular by billowing out as they spin.

Musical instruments
Despite the dramatic visual elements of Beijing Opera, the Chinese say that they go to "listen" to opera, not to see it. Typically six or seven musicians accompany the dramatics. The stringed instruments usually include the *erhu*, or Chinese two-stringed violin, while percussion includes instruments such as clappers, gongs, and drums.

Sheng
There are four main role types in Beijing Opera: *sheng* (male), *dan* (female), *jing* (painted face), and *chou* (clown). *Sheng* are divided into *laosheng*, who wear beards and represent old men, *xiaosheng* who are young men, and *wusheng*, who are the acrobats and whose roles are typically those of warriors.

Dan
Dan are the female roles. *Laodan* are old ladies and *caidan* the female comedians, while *wudan* are the martial artists. The most important category, *qingyi*, usually play respectable and decent ladies in elegant costumes.

Jing
Jing have stylized patterned, colored faces, and represent warriors, heroes, statesmen, adventurers, and demons. Not only are these characters the

most striking looking but they also usually have the most forceful personalities.

Chou
The *chou* are the comic characters and they're denoted by white patches on their noses. Patches of different shape and size mean roles of different character. It is the *chou* who keep the audience laughing.

Mei Lanfang
Mei Lanfang was the foremost male interpreter of the female role *(dan)* during Beijing Opera's heyday in the 1920s and 1930s. Traditionally all female roles were played by male actors, although no longer.

Repertoire
The traditional repertoire includes more than 1,000 works, mostly based on popular tales. Modern productions aimed at tourists often include English-language displays of the text.

Monkey
Clever, resourceful, and brave, Monkey is one of the favorite characters in Beijing Opera. He has his origins in classic Chinese literature.

**Dan (left),
Chou (center),
Monkey (right)**

Top 10 Beijing Opera Venues

1 Beijing Traditional Opera Theater
Highlights shows in English. ⊗ 8 Majiapu Dong Lu, south of Taoranting Park • 6757 2221

2 Chang'an Grand Theater
Daily two-hour performances of mostly complete operas. ⊗ 7 Jianguo Men Nei Dajie • Map G4 • 6510 1309/10

3 Mei Lanfang Grand Theater
This steel-and-glass theater sits over 1,000 people. ⊗ 32 Ping'Anli Xi Dajie • 5833 1388

4 East Pioneer Theater
Occasional two-hour highlights shows. ⊗ 8-2 Dongdan 3 Tiao, off Wangfujing Dajie • Map N4 • 6559 7364

5 Hu Guang Guildhouse
Daily one-hour highlights shows. ⊗ 3 Hufang Lu • Map D5 • 6351 8284

6 Lao She Teahouse
Daily 90-minute variety shows. ⊗ 3 Qian Men Xi Dajie • Map L6 • 6303 6830

7 Li Yuan Theater
Daily 80-minute highlights shows. ⊗ Qian Men Jianguo Hotel, 175 Yong'an Lu • Map D6 • 6301 6688

8 Mansion of Prince Gong
Summer performances only (see p21). ⊗ 17 Qianhai Xi Jie • Map D2 • 8328 8149

9 De Yun She
A famous teahouse hosting traditional Chinese cross-talk shows Tue–Sun. ⊗ 1 Bei Wei Lu • Map E6 • 5165 5060

10 Zheng Yi Temple Theater
Daily two-hour performances. ⊗ 220 Xiheyan Qian Men • Map K6 • 8315 1650

For more on entertainment in Beijing See pp54–5

Beijing's Top 10

Left **National Aquatics Center** Right **National Olympic Stadium**

🔟 The Olympic Legacy

1 National Olympic Stadium (Bird's Nest)

Designed by the Swiss firm Herzog & de Meuron in collaboration with the Chinese artist and architect Ai Weiwei, the National Olympic Stadium has become an architectural icon. Its outer ribbons of structural steel resemble the woven twigs of a bird's nest as they loop and swirl over the 91,000-seat arena, hence the building's nickname.

2 National Aquatics Center/ Water Cube

Inspired by the formation of bubbles and molecules, the Water Cube is a complex of five pools. After the Olympic Games the facility was transformed into a giant water park with slides and a wave pool (see p52).

3 National Indoor Stadium

Built to host gymnastics and handball during the 2008 Games, this stadium boasts a sinuously curving roof with slatted beams, which is inspired by traditional Chinese folding fans. Post-Olympics, the stadium has staged entertainment events and sports competitions.

4 Olympic Green

The Olympic Green surrounds the Olympic Village and extends beyond the fifth ring road, covering a total of 1,680 acres (680 hectares). At its heart is a dragon-shaped lake, as well as waterfalls, meadows, and streams. Entrance into the park is free for all visitors.

5 Olympic Green Convention Center

This building hosted the fencing events during the 2008 Games, as well as providing a home for the International Broadcasting Center. Its distinctive shape mirrors the traditional Chinese "flying roof" and acts as a giant rainwater collector. In 2009 the building reopened as a multi-purpose conference center.

6 Digital Beijing Building

Designed by Beijing-based Studio Pei Zhu, Digital Beijing served as the Games' Control and Data Center. It resembles a bar code from one side and an integrated circuit board from the other. Post-Games, it accommodates a virtual museum and an exhibition center.

7 Beijing Airport, Terminal 3

The world's largest and most advanced airport building, Lord Norman Foster's Terminal 3

Digital Beijing Building

welcomed athletes from around the world to the 2008 Olympics. The design resembles a soaring dragon in red and yellow, thus evoking traditional Chinese colors and symbols.

National Center for the Performing Arts

French architect Paul Andreu's silvery "Egg" *(see p67)* provides a striking contrast to the monolithic, slab-like Socialist architecture of neighboring Tian'an Men Square. The building is surrounded by a reflective moat and accessed by an underwater tunnel. At night, a part of the facade is transparent, so passers-by can see what's going on inside. ✈ *Map K5*

CCTV Building

The most striking addition to the Beijing skyline is the headquarters of China Central Television. Designed by Dutch architects Rem Koolhaas and Ole Scheeren, it is a gravity-defying loop that pushes the limits of architecture and reinvents the organization of spaces. Its unconventional design has prompted some locals to nickname the building "Glass Pants" (trousers). ✈ *Map H4*

MasterCard Center

Rebranded after the 2008 Olympics, the host venue for the basketball competition features a unique exterior design that gives the impression of movement, with boards alternately rising and falling. More than mere show, the aluminum alloy boards reflect heat and reportedly result in 60–70 percent energy savings. Inside, the gymnasium has a capacity to seat 18,000 people and is one of Beijing's largest.

Top 10 Socialist Monuments

1 Agricultural Exhibition Center

In 1959, to celebrate the tenth anniversary of the People's Republic of China, this was one of ten "key" buildings commissioned in "modern" Chinese style. ✈ *Map H2*

2 Great Hall of the People

Over 300 rooms large, yet built in only 10 months. ✈ *Map L5*

3 National Museum of China

Every bit as brutal and ugly as the Great Hall, which it faces across the square. ✈ *Map M5*

4 Beijing Railway Station

Prime illustration of 1959's prevailing "size is everything" approach to architecture. ✈ *Map F4*

5 Cultural Palace of the Nationalities

The one "tenth-anniversary" building of elegance. Its plan forms the Chinese character for "mountain." ✈ *Map C4*

6 Minzu Hotel

No Chinese motifs – but suitably monolithic and drab. ✈ *Map C4*

7 Chinese Military History Museum

Owes a striking debt to Moscow. ✈ *Map A4*

8 Natural History Museum

Neo-Classical Socialist Chinese – but nice inside. ✈ *Map E6*

9 National Art Museum of China

The largest art gallery in China. ✈ *Map M2*

10 Beijing West Railway Station

1995 update on 1959-style architecture. ✈ *Map A5*

Left **Capital Museum** Center **Science and Technology Museum** Right **Beijing Police Museum**

Museums

1 Arthur Sackler Museum
Part of the Beijing University archeology department, this museum has a collection that spans 280,000 years, from the Paleolithic era to the Qing dynasty. As well as fossils and bones, it includes beautiful bronzes and fine ceramics. ◈ *Beijing University campus, Haidian district • 6275 1667 • Open 9am–4pm daily • ¥20 (foreign visitors must bring their passport)*

2 Ancient Architecture Museum
Close to the Temple of Heaven, south of Tian'an Men Square, this place is worth visiting for the museum building alone, which is the pavilion of a former grand temple complex *(see p74)*.

3 Capital Museum
Formerly housed in the Confucius Temple, this museum now boasts a huge, modern five-story building near Fuxingmen. It documents Beijing's history through more than 200,000 relics and archival images. Among the several permanent exhibitions is the fascinating "Stories of the Capital City – Old Beijing Folk Customs" *(see p91)*.

4 Imperial City Museum
After wandering around the Forbidden City, call by this nearby museum to see all the bits of imperial Beijing that didn't survive. The walls and gates that once encircled the city, along with literally dozens of vanished temples, are revisited through a great many maps, models, and photographs *(see p68)*.

5 Military Museum of the Chinese People's Revolution
Visitors to the museum are greeted by paintings of Mao, Marx, Lenin, and Stalin, at least two of whom were fully conversant with the various methods of bringing death and destruction celebrated inside. The ground floor is filled with fighter planes, tanks, and missiles, while displays upstairs chronicle China's military campaigns *(see p91)*.

Military Museum of the Chinese People's Revolution

Natural History Museum

National Museum of China

What the Metropolitan Museum is to New York and the British Museum is to London, the National Museum of China is to Beijing. Dedicated to Chinese history and arts, it documents the evolution of Chinese civilization through the country's most important historic and cultural artifacts. The museum hosts two permanent and numerous temporary exhibitions of art, history, and archaeology *(see p67)*.

National Museum of China

Science and Technology Museum

Exhibits at this suitably hi-tech looking complex start with ancient science and come bang up-to-date with space capsules and magnetic-levitation trains *(see p96)*.

Natural History Museum

There are around 5,000 specimens on display, including a fine collection of models and skeletons of dinosaurs, and other creatures that are even more prehistoric than the Socialist stylings of the museum building *(see p74)*.

Beijing Police Museum

Housed in the 19th-century former City Bank of New York in the old Legation Quarter, this surprisingly fun museum boasts displays on themes such as the suppression of counter-revolutionaries and drug dealers. Famed police dog Feisheng is here – stuffed and mounted – and there are live transmissions from a roadside traffic camera. An interactive screen poses legal questions and correct answers win prizes: it doesn't say what the punishment is for those who answer wrongly. Ⓢ *36 Dong Jiao Min Xiang • Map M6 • 8522 5018 • Subway: Qian Men • Open 9am–4pm Tue–Sun • ¥5*

National Art Museum of China

The largest art museum in the country, with an impressive 64,580 sq ft (6,000 sq m) of floor space, the National Art Museum of China hosts exhibitions by internationally renowned Chinese and foreign artists. Memorable shows have included a themed calligraphy exhibition and a display by Mexican photographer Pedro Meyer *(see p69)*.

→ There are more museums housed in some of the many pavilions of the Forbidden City See pp8–11

Left **Incense sticks for sale** Center **South Cathedral** Right **Cow Street Mosque**

Places of Worship

Lama Temple

South Cathedral
Also known as St. Mary's Church, this was Beijing's first Catholic house of worship. It remains the largest functioning church, and has regular services in a variety of languages including Chinese, English, and Latin. Service times are posted on the noticeboard (see p75).

Cow Street Mosque
There are currently about 200,000 Muslims in Beijing. The majority live in the Niu Jie district, which is where you find this mosque, also known as the Niu Jie Mosque. It is the city's oldest and largest Islamic place of worship. Despite being over one thousand years old, the mosque has been renovated to the tune of $2.4 million and looks splendid (see p74).

Fayuan Temple
This temple doubles as the city's Buddhist Academy. Founded in 1956, the Academy trains monks to serve in monasteries throughout China. The temple has an excellent collection of effigies, including a giant reclining Buddha (see p75).

Lama Temple
Formerly one of the most notable centers of Buddhism outside Tibet until it was shut down during the Cultural Revolution. It was reputedly saved from destruction by the intervention of the president, Zhou Enlai. With Buddhism enjoying a resurgence in popularity, the precincts are once again home to around 70 monks (see pp16–17).

North Cathedral
Not far west of Bei Hai Park, this cathedral is a twin-towered piece of Gothic confectionery, painted in blue with white trim, like a Wedgwood dish. But the bright façade masks a bloody past: not long after the Jesuits finished the church in 1889 it came under siege from the

Main hall, Fayuan Temple

Previous pages **Detail from Nine-dragon Screen, Bei Hai Park**

Boxers during the 1900 rebellion. Many of the congregation sheltering inside were killed. ◉ *Xishiku Dajie* • *Map J2* • *Subway: Xidan*

6 Confucius Temple (Kong Miao)

During the Cultural Revolution, Confucianism was a dirty word, and its temples were converted to other uses, or just abandoned. Recent years have seen a U-turn, with Confucian values being touted anew by Beijing's leaders, but this important temple remains neglected (see p81).

7 Wanshou Temple

Up in the northwest Haidian district, the Wanshou (Longevity) Temple is worth a stop en route to the Summer Palace. Looking not unlike a mini Forbidden City, the complex houses the Beijing Art Museum – a collection of historical relics including bronzes, jade, carved lacquer, and a small but exquisite collection of Buddha images. ◉ *Xisanhuan Lu, on the north side of Zizhu Qiao Bridge* • *Map A1* • *6845 6997* • *Subway: Xizhi Men, then bus 300, 360, or 361* • *Open 9am–4pm Tue–Sun* • *¥20*

8 St. Joseph's Church

Also known as the East Cathedral, this is an attractive triple-domed church in the Baroque style. It was first built on the site of the residence of a Jesuit missionary in 1655 and, following earthquakes, fire, and the destruction wrought during the Boxer Rebellion, has

Confucius Temple

had to be rebuilt on a number of occasions since. It is fronted by a gateway and piazza, and is beautifully lit at night. ◉ *74 Wangfujing Dajie* • *Map N3* • *6524 0634* • *Subway: Dengshikou*

9 White Cloud Temple

Home to the China Daoist Association, the temple was founded in AD 739 and is Beijing's largest Daoist shrine. Daoism, also known as Taoism, is a Chinese folk religion, which centers around maintaining a positive relationship with several categories of gods, ghosts, and ancestral spirits (see p91).

10 St. Michael's Church

One of the city's less well-known churches, St. Michael's is hidden away in the old Legation Quarter (see p75). It was built in 1901, with three spires in Gothic style, to serve the area's various embassies. Narrowly escaping destruction during the Cultural Revolution, it was renovated by the Chinese Patriotic Catholic Church, to whom it now belongs. ◉ *Dong Jiao Min Xiang* • *Map N5* • *Subway: Chongwen Men*

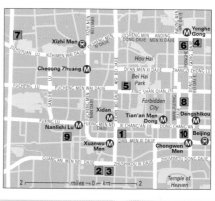

Left **Embroidered silk** Center **Carved stone statues** Right **Tea**

TOP 10 Souvenirs

1 Tea sets
You'll never look at a cup the same way again. For a start, Chinese tea cups are often three-piece affairs with a saucer to prevent burned fingers and a lid to keep the leaves out of your mouth. They are sized from mug to thimble, and the colors and patterning can be exquisite, making a nicely boxed tea set the number one gift from China.

2 Tea
All over Beijing are shops devoted to tea. Malian Dao, a street in the southwest of the city *(see p76)*, has dozens of tea shops offering around 500 different varieties of leaf. The packaging can often be quite beautiful too, from bright red tins to cardboard-tube containers decorated with a waving Mao.

3 Contemporary art
Not just a striking souvenir but also a potential investment. Collecting Chinese art is big

Painted scroll

Chinese tea set

business and some names go for tens of thousands of dollars at international auction. The capital's galleries showcase a wide variety of Chinese artists, but their works may not be particularly affordable.

4 Silk
A Chinese invention and still widely employed today for fine-quality clothing and embroidery. Genuine silk garments are expensive but look out for cheaper household accessories such as silk cushions or bags.

5 Calligraphy
It's a skill that is as revered as painting. Master calligraphers practice their art assiduously, and their works can be very expensive. However, hanging wall scrolls are available at affordable prices and make beautiful souvenirs, especially for anyone with an appropriately Zen-like apartment back home.

6 Marble chops
A chop is a signature, carved onto wood, marble, stone, or plastic, and used as a stamp on official documents or contracts. It is impossible to do business in China without a chop. You can quickly and easily get your own by having your name translated into Chinese characters and taking it along to a chop-maker.

7 Mao memorabilia
The great icon Mao appears on posters, badges, banners, and almost anything else with a flat surface. There are shops and stalls that trade in nothing but Mao in the Dazhalan district and at Panjiayuan Market.

8 Ceramics
China has been producing ceramics for centuries. The finest come from Jingdezhen, and can be seen at Ceramic City at 277 Wangfujing Dajie. Just remember, you have to get it home in one piece.

9 Lanterns and lamps
The beautiful red lanterns that you see hanging all over Beijing make a fantastic and very affordable souvenir of China. An equally attractive variant are the table lamps with distinctive red, tulip-shaped shades. These should cost no more than a few yuan.

10 Designer clothing
Hottest souvenirs from Beijing are top-label international brands, sold here for a fraction of the cost back home. They are all, of course, fakes – almost passable copies but poorer quality. Those whose copyrights are being infringed have begun to take legal action and the days of the fakes may be numbered.

Mao memorabilia

Top 10 Galleries

1 798 Space
For contemporary art, the place to go is the 798 Art District. This is the gallery that started it all *(see p24)*.
www.798space.com

2 Boers-Li
A high-profile gallery with two exhibition spaces.
www.boersligallery.com

3 Red Gate Gallery
Art in a 15th-century city watchtower *(see p85)*.
www.redgategallery.com

4 PKM Gallery
A Seoul-based gallery with one of the largest spaces in Caochangdi.
www.pkmgallery.com

5 Galleria Continua
The Beijing outpost of this Italian gallery is located in the 798 District *(see p25)*.
www.galleriacontinua.com

6 Pace Beijing
This New York City gallery's outpost in the 798 Art District focuses on Chinese art.
www.pacebeijing.com

7 UCCA
One of 798 District's largest and most acclaimed contemporary art galleries *(see p25)*. www.ucca.org.cn

8 Urs Meile
A gallery founded by Swiss art dealer Urs Meile in a space designed by Ai Wei Wei.
www.galerieursmeile.com

9 Pekin Fine Arts
Innovative art space at Caochangdi promoting new Asian artists *(see p25)*.
www.pekinfinearts.com

10 Courtyard Gallery
This gallery has locations on Dong'anmen Dajie, as well as an annex in a converted factory in Caochangdi.
www.courtyard-gallery.com

For Beijing's Top 10 markets and malls See pp50–51

Left **Hong Qiao Market** Right **Panjiayuan Antique Market**

Markets and Malls

Oriental Plaza

third main tourist attraction after the Forbidden City and the Great Wall. Some 100,000 shoppers a day visit to snap up famous brand goods for ridiculously low prices. Of course, they are all fakes, but who's to know? Come prepared for feisty salespeople and items of varying quality *(see p88)*.

Hong Qiao Market

Hong Qiao is best known for pearls (hence its alternative name, the "Pearl Market"), with a huge range available, freshwater and seawater, up on the third floor. The floors below are a tight compress of clothing, shoes, electronics, and more, while in the basement is a pungent, but fascinating market for fish, frogs, and snakes *(see p76)*.

Oriental Plaza

A large mall that stretches a whole city block and boasts several levels of top-end retailers including Paul Smith, Swarovski, Sisley, Max Mara, and Apple. There is also a Watsons drugstore, a big CD and DVD store, and an excellent food court *(see p70)*.

Silk Market

More properly known as Xiushui, this is the most infamous market in Beijing. It is reportedly the city's

Yashow Market

At the center of the embassy district of Sanlitun, Yashow offers more of the same as the Silk Market: four floors of clothing, bags, shoes, and sportswear, plus some jewelry, nail salons, and a bunch of tailors on the top floor. You may find that vendors here are less aggressive than at the Silk Market *(see p88)*.

Panjiayuan Antique Market

As much a tourist attraction as a shopping experience, Panjiayuan is home to around 3,000 dealers peddling everything from broken

Beijing shopper

bicycles to family heirlooms. Come here for Mao memorabilia, a Qing-dynasty vase, or yellowing Tintin comics in Chinese. Panjiayuan Market is at its busiest, best, and most chaotic at the weekends. Serious collectors swoop at dawn, but it's fun any time *(see p76)*.

6 China World Shopping Mall and Shin Kong Plaza

The CBD around Guomao is China's equivalent of Wall Street, attracting luxury hotels as well as glitzy malls. China World and Shin Kong are both home to high-end international brands such as Louis Vuitton, Prada, and Moschino. Prices are at least as high as back home (see p88).

7 Dong Jiao Wholesale Market

In a series of hangar-like buildings southeast of SOHO, traders sell just about anything. This is where restaurants and hotels buy pots and pans, schools come for classroom supplies, service staff buy uniforms, and small traders and cooks come for fresh fruit and vegetables. You may not need a carton of 1,000 chopsticks, but it is fascinating to browse, all the same. ◈ Dong Si Huan Zhong Lu, west of Sihui Bridge • Map G4 • Subway: Guomao • Open daily

8 The Village Sanlitun

This hip shopping, dining, and entertainment center in Sanlitun features numerous colored glass buildings housing over 200 stores, including global brand flagships such as the Apple Store and Nike, plus some of downtown Beijing's best bars and cafés (see p88).

9 Solana

Located next to Chaoyang Park, Solana is Beijing's biggest outdoor shopping mall. It is a California-style complex centered around a plaza with fountains, a clock tower, and paths leading to a lakeside strip. Zara, Esprit, Nike, and Sephora are some of the brands you can find here;

Bead stall at Yashow Market

Todai is a popular eatery famed for its sushi and seafood buffet. ◈ 6 Chaoyang Park Road • 5905 6666 • Open 11am–9pm daily

10 Zhongguancun, Electronics Avenue

Zhongguancun is the capital's technology hub, and Electronics Avenue is home to some of the biggest electronics markets in Beijing. Stores sell everything from computers and mp3 players to cameras. Staff rarely speak English, so bring a printout of the model you want. ◈ Subway: Wudaokou, then taxi

Beaded purse

Left **Natural History Museum** Center **China Ethnic Culture Park** Right **At play in the park**

🔟 Children's Attractions

1 Water Cube

The 2008 Olympics Aquatic Center is now a themed water park for kids that adults will also enjoy. Water slides and pipes and giant inflatable rides will excite young water fans, while the Bullet Bowl "plug hole" descent on a four-seater dinghy is a thrill for any age. ⊗ *Olympic Park, 11 Tianchen Donglu, Chaoyang District • 8437 0112 • Subway: Olympic Sports Center • Open 10am–9pm daily • adults ¥200; children ¥160; under 4 ft (1.2 m) free*

2 Beijing Zoo

Most children will remain happily oblivious to the poor conditions that many of the animals are kept in and which are likely to upset older animal lovers. However, the pandas are well cared for and the setting is pleasant and leafy *(see p92).*

3 Beijing Aquarium

Located in the northeastern corner of the zoo, this is a very impressive attraction that will

Pandas at Beijing Zoo

keep children happy for hours, especially the dolphin shows *(see p92).*

4 Fundazzle

Fundazzle is a massive indoor kids' playground. Loud and bright, it has a two-story jungle gym, a vast plastic ball-filled pool, trampolines, swings, and a host of other activities and enticements with which to reward young children who've just had to endure hours of being dragged round the Forbidden City. ⊗ *Gongren Tiyuchang Nan Lu, south side of Workers' Stadium • Map G3 • 6593 6208 • Subway: Chaoyang Men • Open 9am–5pm Mon–Fri, 9am–7pm Sat & Sun • ¥35 for 2 hrs*

5 Natural History Museum

As long as you steer them clear of the horror show that is the exhibit of partially dissected human bodies, children will love the giant animatronic dinosaurs and prehistoric skeletons, as well as the plethora of stuffed animals of all species and sizes *(see p74).*

6 China Ethnic Culture Park

Like an overgrown model village, "China World" is filled with colorful models of buildings representing all the nation's many and varied ethnic minorities. Some of the models are huge, and it's all very colorful, as are the regular performances by ethnic musicians and singers in full costume *(see p96).*

➡ *Check out the monthly* Beijing Kids *magazine (www.beijing-kids. com) for up-to-date events*

Beijing Aquarium at Beijing Zoo

Blue Zoo Beijing

7 Not to be confused with Beijing Zoo, this is a small but beautifully done aquarium. It has an enormous coral reef tank containing an array of visually exciting marine life, including eels, rays, and sharks. A big plus is that the tanks are set low enough that toddlers can peer into them. There's also a "marine tunnel" and twice-daily shark-feeding sessions (see p86).

Science and Technology Museum

8 Lots of hands-on and interactive exhibits for children to pull, push, and even walk through. There is also an IMAX-style movie theater and an indoor play area on the third and fourth floors of a separate building north of the main entrance (see p96).

Happy Valley

9 Disneyland-style theme park divided into six themed regions, with 120 attractions. The park's aim is to keep both parents and children content by providing interactive education experiences. Thrill-seekers can enjoy no fewer than 40 rides,

of which ten are "extreme," including a "Drop Tower" in which riders fall at 45 mph (72 km/h) in a terrifying simulated plunge to earth. There is also a shopping complex, and an IMAX cinema. ◎ *Xiaowuji Bei Lu, East 4th Ring Road • 6738 3333 • Open 9:30am–10pm daily • adults ¥200; children ¥130; under 4 ft (1.2 m) free*

New China Children's Store

10 A four-storied children's store on Beijing's main shopping street, with everything from carry cots and strollers to masses of local and imported toys. There's even an in-store play area. ◎ *168 Wangfujing Dajie • Map N4 • 6528 1774 • Subway: Wangfujing • Open 9am–9:30pm daily*

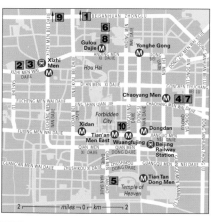

Most Chinese restaurants tend to be children friendly. The Bookworm in Sanlitun has a children's reading corner. See p61

53

Left **Rock at the Workers' Gymnasium** Right **Football at the Workers' Stadium**

🔟 Entertainment

1 Acrobatics

China has a worldwide reputation for its gymnasts, who perform breathtaking routines that showcase their unnerving flexibility. Displays of balance often involve props such as chairs, plates, and bicycles. Several Beijing theaters put on shows – for instance, the Tianqiao Acrobatics Theater in Xuanwu; your hotel will be able to help with reservations.

Beijing Opera performer

2 Beijing Opera

With its incomprehensible plots, unfamiliar sounds, and performances lasting up to three hours, Beijing Opera is a hard-to-acquire taste. However, everyone should try it at least once *(see pp38–9)*.

Acrobatic show

3 Cinema

The low cost and widespread availability of pirate DVDs means that most Beijingers stay home to watch their movies. Publicly screened films are subject to censorship, but a few venues and foreign cultural institutes host screenings of independent and classic films. For the latest movies, head to Wanda Cineplex.

4 Classical music

Attend a Chinese orchestral performance if possible. Sections of unfamiliar plucked string, bowed string, woodwind, and percussion instruments compete for attention in swirling arrangements. The main venues are the Forbidden City Concert Hall in Zhong Shan Park and the National Center for the Performing Arts *(see p67)*.

5 Martial arts

The Shaolin monks from Songshan in Henan Province have gained an international reputation for their martial arts prowess. They perform regularly at the Li Yuan Theater *(see p39)*.

6 Puppet theater

Shadow-puppet theater is an art form that has been performed more or less unchanged in China since the 3rd century AD. Shows employ many of the story lines and musical styles of Beijing

Opera, while the puppets can be quite elaborate and colorfully dressed. The best place to catch a performance is at the China Puppet Art Theater (Anhua Xili, off Bei Sanhuan Lu).

7 Rock and pop
Beijing is the Chinese city with all the best tunes. It has a thriving music scene supported by a host of small music bars and clubs (see p63). Punk and metal thrive, but of far more interest are local folk rockers who mix ethnic instrumentation with Western genres.

8 Sports
Football is big in Beijing. The local boys are Beijing Guo'an, who play in the China Super League at the Workers' Stadium (see p86). Tickets are easy to find: you can just show up at the stadium on game day. Second in popularity is basketball. The top team is Aoshen, which plays at the Beijing Guang'an Gymnasium (Baiguang Lu; Map C6).

9 Teahouses
You shouldn't leave Beijing without visiting a teahouse. Tea is served with great ceremony, complete with smellings and recitations of Confucian sayings and poetry. The price of the tea varies greatly according to quality. For venues, see p59.

10 Theater
Beijing is home to several excellent theaters, where a few established troupes perform regularly. Canonical works such as Lao She's "Teahouse" are increasingly supplemented by big-budget Western musicals such as "Rent" and "Aladdin on Ice". See the English-language press for what's on.

Top 10 Chinese Movies

1 Beijing Bicycle
(Wang Xiaoshuai; 2001) A young bike messenger has his ride stolen and attempts to get it back.

2 Spring in a Small Town
(Fei Mu; 1948) A man returns home to find his childhood sweetheart married. Voted best Chinese film of all time.

3 Yellow Earth
(Chen Kaige; 1984) A Red Army soldier is posted to a desolate province to collect folk songs and finds misery.

4 Still Life
(Jia Zhangke; 2006) A powerful film about the upheaval resulting from the Three Gorges Project.

5 Lust, Caution
(Ang Lee; 2007) A thriller set in pre-World War II Shanghai, adapted from a novella by Eileen Chang.

6 A Touch of Zen
(King Hu; 1969) Sword-play films have been popular in China since the 1920s, but this revitalized the genre.

7 Raise the Red Lantern
(Zhang Yimou; 1991) Intrigue between the multiple wives of a wealthy overlord.

8 Farewell My Concubine
(Chen Kaige; 1993) The film that really put Chinese cinema back on the map.

9 Hero
(Zhang Yimou; 2002) Martial arts waltz that to date is the most successful film ever made in China.

10 In the Mood for Love
(Wong Kar-wai; 2000) Set in 1960s Hong Kong, this cool thriller launched its stars Tony Leung and Maggie Cheung onto the international film scene.

Left **Tea being poured in a Beijing restaurant** Center **Lamb and scallions** Right **Dumplings**

🔟 Beijing Dishes

Beijing duck

1 Beijing duck
The best-known dish in north Chinese cuisine. The duck, a local Beijing variety, is dried and brushed with a sweet marinade before being roasted over fragrant wood chips. It is carved by the chef and eaten wrapped in pancakes with slivered scallions (spring onions) and cucumber.

2 Hotpot
Introduced to Beijing in the 13th century by the invading Mongols, hotpot is a much-loved staple. Literally hundreds of restaurants across the city sell nothing else but. It's a great group dish, with everybody sat around a large bubbling pot of broth dropping in their own shavings of meat, noodles, and vegetables to cook.

3 Zha jiang mian
The name means "clanging dish noodles" – like hot pot, ingredients are added at the table to a central tureen of noodles, and the bowls are loudly clanged together as each dish goes in, hence the name.

4 Jiaozi
The traditional Beijing dumplings are filled with pork, *bai cai* (Chinese leaf), and ginger but, in fact, fillings are endless. You can find *jiaozi* at snack shops all over the city. They are also sold on the street, served from a giant hot plate over a brazier.

5 Thousand-year-old eggs
These are raw duck eggs that have been put into mud, chalk and ammonia and left, not for a thousand years, but more like two weeks. When retrieved, the egg is steamed or hard-boiled: the white has turned a greenish-black. The eggs are cut up and sprinkled with soy sauce and sesame oil.

6 Lao mian
Watching a cook make *lao mian* (hand-pulled noodles) is almost as enjoyable as eating

Hotpot

For Beijing's best Chinese restaurants **See pp58–9**

Sweet and sour carp

them. First the dough is stretched and then swung like a skipping rope, so that it becomes plaited. The process is repeated until the strands of dough are as thin as string.

7 Lamb and scallions
Scallions (spring onions) are a common Beijing ingredient and in this dish they are rapidly stir-fried along with sliced lamb, garlic, and a sweet-bean paste.

8 Sweet and sour carp
Beijing cooking is heavily influenced by the cuisine of Shandong Province, generally regarded as the oldest and best in China. Sweet and sour carp is a quintessential Shandong dish traditionally made with fish from the Yellow River.

9 Drunken empress chicken
Supposedly named after Yang Guifei, an imperial concubine overly fond of her alcohol. The dish is prepared using Chinese wine and is served cold.

10 Stir-fried kidney flowers
These are actually pork kidneys cut in a criss-cross fashion and stir-fried, during which they open out like "flowers". The kidneys are typically prepared with bamboo shoots, water chestnuts, and edible black fungus (a sort of mushroom).

Top 10 Beijing Street Foods

1 Lu da gun'r
Literally "donkeys rolling in dirt": sweet red-bean paste in a rice dough dusted with peanut powder.

2 Jian bing
Chinese crêpe. Often sold off the back of tricycles and a typical Beijing breakfast.

3 Shao bing
Hot bread roll sometimes filled with a fried egg and often sprinkled with aniseed for flavoring.

4 Tang chao lizi
Chestnuts, roasted in sugar and hot sand and served in a paper bag. A seasonal snack appearing in autumn.

5 Tang hu lu
A kabob of candied hawthorn berries.

6 Chuan'r
In any area with lots of bars and clubs you'll find street vendors selling *chuan'r* (kabobs). They cost just a few *yuan* per skewer.

7 Baozi
These delicious steamed dumplings are cooked in bamboo baskets. Typical fillings include pork, chicken, beef, or vegetables and tofu.

8 Rou bing
Cooked bread filled with finely chopped and spiced pork. A variant is *rou jiamo*, which is a bun filled with diced lamb.

9 You tiao
Deep-fried dough sticks, often dipped in warm congee (a rice porridge).

10 Hong shu
A winter specialty, these are baked sweet potatoes, often heated in ovens made from oil drums.

Beijing's Top 10

 Check the local press for details of cooking classes

Left **Bellagio** Right **Beijing Dadong Roast Duck Restaurant**

Chinese Restaurants

Hakka foil-baked fish dish

1 Beijing Dadong Roast Duck Restaurant

Lots of restaurants specialize in Beijing's most famous dish, and debate rages endlessly over who serves the best fowl. This place is less over-blown and over-priced than many of its rivals, and for that it gets our vote *(see p89)*.

2 Dali Courtyard

Beautifully lit by candles at night, this atmospheric courtyard venue wins top marks for ambience, as well as for its excellent set menus made up of classic dishes from Yunnan province. It's a good idea to reserve a table *(see p83)*.

3 Three Guizhou Men

Authentic Guizhou food, uncompromisingly spicy and sour, is generally too coarse for foreign tastes, but here it is blended with more conventional Chinese flavors. The atmosphere is stylish, in keeping

with the local hipster fondness for minority cuisines. ◎ *6 Guanghua Xili • Map G4 • 6502 1733 • ¥¥*

4 Duck de Chine

The wood-fired roast duck here has garnered numerous awards. It is served with a distinctive French twist as well as in the signature Beijing style. ◎ *1949 The Hidden City Courtyard 4, Gongren Tiyuchang Bei Lu • Map H2 • 6501 8881 • ¥¥¥*

5 Bellagio

A supremely hip and stylish Taiwanese chain, also serving quality Hakka dishes. Everything looks stunning, and it tastes even better. Leave room for one of the hugely popular red-bean ice desserts *(see p89)*.

6 Made In China

The kitchen is open allowing diners to view ducks roasting and nimble fingers speedily making disks of dough and spooning in fragrant fillings to make the little dumplings known as *jiaozi*, a Beijing specialty *(see p56 and p71)*.

Made In China

7 Transit

The spicy hotpots of Sichuan province are very popular in Beijing, and this restaurant puts a smart twist on regional dining. Their authentic, pepper-laden dishes are beautifully flavored *(see p89)*.

Preparing Beijing duck

Cuisine Cuisine

Sample Cantonese *haute cuisine* at this lavishly decorated mainland offshoot of Hong Kong's original Michelin-starred restaurant. It offers a modern take on Cantonese classic dishes in an ornate settting. ◈ *2/F West Tower, WFC, 1 Dongsanhuan Zhong Lu* • *Map H3* • *5891 7626* • ¥¥¥

Huang Ting

A beautiful restaurant: a recreation of a traditional *siheyuan* (courtyard) house reusing thousands of bricks from demolished properties, along with wooden screens, carved stone friezes, and door guardian stones. Dishes lean toward the Cantonese, but there are also Beijing favorites, including classic Beijing roast duck (see p56 and p71).

Tiandi

Equally appealing to the palate as to the eyes, the Imperial-style dishes here are truly fit for an emperor. Diners feast surrounded by sumptuous Ming dynasty antique furniture, while tables are dotted around picturesque koi ponds. And it's all within a short walk of the Forbidden City (see p71).

Top 10 Teahouses

1 Samwei Bookstore Teahouse
A relaxed place with cultural and musical events. ◈ *60 Fuxing Men Dajie (opposite the Minzu Hotel)* • *Map C4*

2 Confucius Teahouse
Just across from the Confucius Temple. English spoken. ◈ *28 Guozijian Lu* • *Map F1*

3 Fu Family Teahouse
A stylish teahouse on the south bank of picturesque Hou Hai (see p82).

4 Hong Hao Ge
Bamboo decor beside a park behind the Military Museum. ◈ *9–12 Yuyuan Tan Nan Lu* • *Map A4*

5 Lao She Teahouse
Tea plus acrobatics, magic tricks, and Beijing Opera. ◈ *3 Qian Men Xi Dajie* • *Map K6*

6 Ming Ren Teahouse
A chain of teahouses; this branch is conveniently close to Hou Hai. ◈ *Building 3, Ping'an Dajie* • *Map K1*

7 Ming Hui Chayuan
Away from the center, but worth the trip for the classic *oolong* and *pu'er* teas. ◈ *Dajue Temple, Bei'an He*

8 Xi Hua Yuan Teahouse
Decorated with ornate Qing-style furniture. Just over the road from the Purple Vine. ◈ *Bei Chang Jie* • *Map L4*

9 Ji Gu Ge Teahouse
Popular teahouse in area of antique shops south of Tian'an Men Square. ◈ *132–6 Liulichang Dongjie* • *Map D5*

10 Tian Qiao Happy Teahouse
Tea ceremonies with food and bite-sized cultural morsels at the upstairs theater. ◈ *1 Bei Wei Lu* • *Map E6*

For more on the different Chinese dishes found in Beijing's restaurants See pp56–7

Left **Capital M** Right **Cafe Sambal**

Top 10 International Restaurants

Temple Restaurant

Temple Restaurant
Located in a beautifully restored 600-year-old temple complex, this upmarket restaurant offers high-quality European cuisine. Advance booking is essential. ✆ 23 Songzhusi Shatan Bei Dajie • Map E3 • 8400 2232 • Subway: Dong Si Shi Tiao

Cafe Sambal
Sambal, a sauce made with chillies, features on the menu at this stylish Malay restaurant, along with other Southeast Asian specialties. The food is complemented by a beautiful courtyard-house setting (see p83).

Hatsune
Hatsune has a dedicated following for its beautiful sushi rolls, prepared with fresh fish flown from Japan. Despite its gorgeous looks and superlative service, it is a lot cheaper than you might imagine (see p89).

Bei
Inspired by the cuisines of North China, Japan, and Korea, this elegant restaurant specializes in a wide range of sushi, sashimi, and prime meat cuts. The food is meticulously prepared and beautifully presented for a well-heeled clientele willing to pay the relatively high prices for assured quality. Reservations recommended (see p89).

Capital M
Housed at a prestigious address that offers a stellar view over Tian'an Men Square, this excellent contemporary restaurant, run by well-known Australian restaurateur Michelle Garnault, never fails to impress (see p77).

Maison Boulud
The Maison Boulud enjoys a sophisticated and stylish setting in the former American Legation building. The cooking is French haute cuisine with an Asian twist and, as you might expect from chef Daniel Boulud's only Chinese outpost, the food is expensive but flawless. Smart dress required (see p77).

Hatsune

Mosto

Nuage
7 The setting is a two-story wooden mansion on the banks of Qian Hai, overlooking the lake. The Vietnamese food is variable but as a romantic night-time dining spot this takes some beating *(see p83)*.

Jing
8 A modernist restaurant dominated by a vast gleaming open kitchen. Watching a team of chefs searing, caramelizing, and flash-frying is a sure way to build up an appetite. The wine list is exemplary *(see p71)*.

Mosto
9 With contemporary international classics served in a buzzy Sanlitun location, this bistro has plenty of fans thanks to its immaculate service and great wine list. ◈ *81 Sanlitun Bei Lu* • *Map H2* • *5208 6030* • *Subway: Tuanjiehu*

Susu
10 Housed in a renovated courtyard building, this stylish restaurant offers authentic Vietnamese dishes created by two Saigon-born chefs. There is a good range of vegetarian options. ◈ *10 Xi Xiang, Qianliang Hutong* • *Map F2* • *8400 2699* • *Subway: Dong Si Shi Tiao*

Top 10 Places to Snack

1 ### Mr Shi's
Popular for pan-fried and steamed pork, shrimp, and vegetarian dumplings. ◈ *74 Baochao Hutong* • *Map E1*

2 ### Xiao Xin's Café
A friendly, bohemian café offering homemade cakes, muffins, and free Wi-Fi. ◈ *103 Nan Luogu Xiang* • *Map E2*

3 ### The Rug Café
Excellent coffee, salads, bagels, and some Chinese dishes. ◈ *1/F, Building 4, Chaoyang Gongyuan Nan Lu*

4 ### The Bookworm
Lending library, bar, and a great place for healthy, light lunches. ◈ *Building 4, Sanlitun Nan Lu* • *Map H2*

5 ### Element Fresh
Hip café serving gourmet salads, smoothies, pastas, and Asian plates. ◈ *Building 8, 19 Sanlitun Lu* • *Map H2*

6 ### Vineyard Café
A great spot on weekends for a full English breakfast. ◈ *31 Wudaoying Hutong* • *Map F1*

7 ### AT Café
Quirky café in the 798 Art District with a limited but appealing menu *(see p24)*.

8 ### Du Yichu
Age-old restaurant that specializes in *baozi* (steamed buns). ◈ *36 Qian Men Dajie, corner of Dazhalan Jie* • *Map E5*

9 ### Wangfujing Snack Street
Kabob, noodle, and soup stalls fill a narrow alley off the bottom end of Wangfujing Dajie. ◈ *Map M4*

10 ### Café Zarah
German-style breakfasts and a wonderful view of Gulou Dong Dajie. ◈ *42 Gulou Dong Dajie* • *Map E2*

Left **No Name Bar** Center **Migas** Right **Centro**

TOP10 Bars and Pubs

1 Bed Tapas & Bar
The perfect Beijing bar – an old courtyard house kitted out with antique furniture, including *kang*-style beds. Excellent food, plus weekend DJs *(see p82)*.

2 Centro
Beijing's classiest bar is off the lobby of one of the city's swankiest hotels. Louche and loungey, it boasts live jazz, sexy waitresses, and the last word in cocktails. ◈ *Kerry Center Hotel, 1 Guanghua Lu • Map H4 • 6561 8833 ext. 6296 • Subway: Guomao*

3 No Name Bar
The oldest Hou Hai bar is also the best, with a ramshackle charm that defeats the copyists. Heated by wood-burning stoves, or cooled by lake breezes, it's perfect year-round *(see p82)*.

4 Mai
A smartly designed cocktail bar, Mai has outdoor seating in a narrow courtyard, plus a giant silver sofa and bar chairs inside. It draws a cool *hutong* crowd, especially at weekends *(see p82)*.

Mai

Bed Tapas & Bar

5 Migas
This chic Spanish restaurant and rooftop terrace bar is always packed with a hip cocktail-drinking crowd that comes here for the live DJs and great alfresco views. ◈ *6/F Nali Patio, 81 Sanlitun Bei Lu • Map H2 • 5208 6061 • Subway: Tuanjiehu*

6 Apothecary
The largest selection of classic and contemporary cocktails in the capital can be found at this casual cocktail bar. It also serves inventive creole-influenced light dishes and small tapas. ◈ *3/F Nali Patio, 81 Sanlitun Bei Lu • Map H2 • 5208 6040 • Subway: Tuanjiehu*

7 D. Lounge
Some say this is the coolest bar in Beijing, and it's hard to disagree once you've tried the fantastically innovative

drinks and the New York-style industrial-chic setting. The venue attracts the "it" crowd and the doormen have been known to restrict entry to the well-dressed. ✆ *Sanlitun Nan Lu* • *Map H2* • *6593 7710* • *Subway: Tuanjiehu*

Bali Courtyard Bar
Styled like a Southeast Asian beach bar and located on a rooftop, this sleek, hipster hangout has comfortable chairs and lounge beds plus strong cocktail mixes and live DJ sets at weekends. ✆ *7/F Zhongyu Plaza, 6 Gongren Tiyuchang Bei Lu* • *Map H2* • *5975 2688* • *Subway: Tuanjiehu*

The Tree
A huge favorite among the city's expats, this is a convivial, stone-floored pub that marries a fantastic array of beers (40 Belgian brews alone) with excellent wood-fired pizzas. ✆ *43 Sanlitun Bei Jie* • *Map H2* • *6415 1954* • *Subway: Dong Si Shi Tiao*

Mesh
Within the ultra-trendy Opposite House boutique hotel, Mesh is a smart lounge bar with a cool outdoor deck terrace and bamboo garden. It's a popular spot for after-work cocktails and pre-party evening drinks on weekends. ✆ *B1, The Opposite House, 11 Sanlitun Bei Lu* • *Map H2* • *6417 6688* • *Subway: Tuanjiehu*

Mesh

Top 10 Music Bars

1 2 Kolegas Bar
Live music bar at a drive-in movie theater. Two miles east of the Lufthansa Center. ✆ *21 Liang Ma Qiao Lu* • *6436 8998*

2 Destination
Eclectic live music venue and club. ✆ *7 Gongti Xi Lu* • *6552 8180*

3 Fez
Mediterranean-themed bar serving wines, cocktails, and Spanish tapas. ✆ *81 Sanlitun Bei Lu* • *Map H2* • *5208 6138*

4 Haze
Stages live music and DJs. ✆ *22 Guanghua Lu SOHO*

5 Dada
Super-hip DJ lounge and mini club import from Shanghai. ✆ *206 Gulou Dong Dajie* • *Map E2* • *183 1108 0818*

6 Mao Live House
This vast, warehouse-like space with a great stage is backed by a Japanese record label. ✆ *111 Gulou Dong Dajie* • *Map E2* • *6402 5080*

7 Modernista
A 1920s-themed jazz and piano bar that also shows artsy European movies and serves Spanish tapas *(see p82)*.

8 The Tree
The music is incidental to the business of drinking, but the occasional act impresses *(see left)*.

9 What? Bar
Terrific little, indie-oriented music bar close by the west gate of the Forbidden City. ✆ *72 Bei Chang Jie* • *Map L3* • *133 4112 2757*

10 Yugong Yishan
The city's most satisfying music venue, with an eclectic but always laudable booking policy. ✆ *3-2 Zhangzizhong Lu* • *6404 2711*

 Beijing's bars are normally open from around noon until 2am

AROUND TOWN

BEIJING'S TOP 10

参观
参观珍宝
购票时间:8:30–
8:30–

NOTICE TO
THE HALL OF
ADMISSION BY TICKET
TICKET BOOKING H
8:30–
8:30–

Tian'an Men Square

Tian'an Men Square and the Forbidden City

THE GEOGRAPHICAL, SPIRITUAL, AND HISTORICAL *heart of Beijing, Tian'an Men Square and the Forbidden City together represent a yin and yang arrangement; one is a mind-bogglingly vast, empty, rectangular public space, the other is an even more massive, rectangular walled private enclosure. One represents modern China, complete with its Socialist monuments, refrigerated Great Leader, and resonances of political upheaval, while the other is a silent repository of ancient imperial glories. There is enough to see around the square and in the Forbidden City to make it worth setting aside a whole day for each. One day will present a vivid impression of China as it was, and the other an equally striking portrait of the country as it is now. And after all that, wander around the corner for a look at the National Center for the Performing Arts and a glimpse of the China of the future.*

Mao's Mausoleum

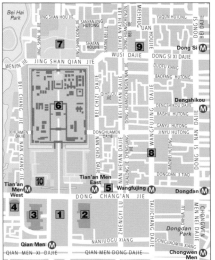

Sights

1. Tian'an Men Square
2. National Museum of China
3. Great Hall of the People
4. National Center for the Performing Arts
5. Imperial City Museum
6. Forbidden City
7. Jing Shan Park
8. Wangfujing Dajie
9. National Art Museum of China
10. Zhong Shan Park

Previous pages Tiled gateway at the Forbidden City

Tian'an Men Square

Although now thoroughly synonymous with Beijing, until relatively recently there was no Tian'an Men Square. For centuries this was just a main thoroughfare leading to the Gate of Heavenly Peace (Tian'an Men) and the approach to the Forbidden City. The area was cleared in the first half of the 20th century, then quadrupled in size in 1959, supposedly allowing for up to one million people to gather. Many of the buildings flanking the square were erected at this time (see pp14–15).

National Museum of China

This huge museum combines the original Museum of Chinese History and the Museum of the Revolution. Of the two, the contents of the former are by far the more interesting, with an unsurpassed collection of great works of Chinese art and other historical, archaeological, and cultural objects. There are also models, documents, and photographs connected with the history of the Chinese Communist Party – for political enthusiasts only. The museum also hosts temporary exhibitions. ⊗ East side of Tian'an Men Square • Map M5 • 6511 6400 • Subway: Tian'an Men East • Open 9am–5pm Tue–Sun • www.chnmuseum.cn

Great Hall of the People

Great Hall of the People

This is the Chinese parliament building, home of the nation's legislative body, the National People's Congress. Regular tours visit the banquet room where US President Nixon dined in 1972 and the 10,000-seat auditorium with its ceiling inset with a massive red star. The building is closed to the public when the Congress is in session. ⊗ West side of Tian'an Men Square • Map L5 • 6605 6847 • Subway: Tian'an Men West • Opening hours vary • ¥30

National Center for the Performing Arts

This modern opera house hosts a year-round program of opera, theater, and concerts, and is a major landmark on Beijing's skyline. Designed by French architect Paul Andreu, it is built of glass and titanium and takes the form of a giant parabolic dome – earning it the nickname "The Egg." Entrance to the building is through an underwater tunnel. ⊗ 2 West Chang An Jie • Map K5 • 6655 0000 • Subway: Tian'an Men West • www.chncpa.org

Tian'an Men traffic policeman

National Center for the Performing Arts

For more modern architecture See pp40–41

The cult of Mao

Mao was an ideologue whose impatience at the pace of reform often brought disaster. Skilful maneuvering by the Party meant that he remained a heroic figure. The years after his death saw a diminishing of his status, as Mao's influence was overshadowed by the political and economic reforms embraced by Deng Xiaoping and other leaders.

Imperial City Museum

Much of the Imperial City of Beijing was destroyed under the Communists. A model in the museum illustrates the extent of what has been lost, including the wall that once encircled the city, the gates, and a great many temples. There are also exhibits on the *hutongs*, plus collections of armor, weapons, and ceramics. ✆ 9 Changpu Heyan • Map M5 • 8511 5104 • Subway: Tian'an Men East • Open 10am–5:30pm Tue–Sun • ¥20 • Audio tour ¥50

Wangfujing street sculptures

Forbidden City

The Forbidden City is Beijing's top "must-see" sight. A seemingly endless collection of pavilions, gates, courts, and gardens, the complex encompasses five centuries of colorful, occasionally lurid, imperial history. Trying to see everything in one go will bring on a severe case of Ming fatigue, and it is recommended that you tackle the palace over at least two visits *(see pp8–11)*.

Jing Shan Park

Jing Shan (Coal Hill) lies immediately north of the Forbidden City. The hill was created from the earth that was excavated while building the moat around the palace complex during the reign of the Ming Yongle emperor. The hill's purpose was to protect the emperor and his court from malign northern influences, which brought death and destruction according to classical *feng shui*. The park is dotted with pavilions and halls, but the highlight is the superb view south over the Forbidden City from the hill-top Wancheng Pavilion. ✆ 1 Wenjin Jie • Map L2 • 6404 4071 • Bus: 5, 111, 124, 810 • Open 6am–9pm daily • ¥2

Wangfujing Dajie

Beijing's main shopping street is filled with department stores and giant malls *(see p70)*, as well as stores selling silk, tea,

Left **Forbidden City** Right **Wangfujing Dajie shopping street**

National Art Museum of China

and shoes. Another highlight is the Night Market, with its range of open-air food stalls (see p71). A little to the north is St. Joseph's, one of the city's most important churches (see p47). ✎ Map N4
• Subway: Wangfujing • Night Market: Open 5:30pm–10pm daily

9 National Art Museum of China

The largest art gallery in China was one of ten key buildings erected in 1959 to celebrate the tenth anniversary of the founding of the People's Republic. It has no permanent collection, but its 14 halls, spread over three floors, host a constant rotation of temporary exhibitions of Chinese and international art. ✎ 1 Wusi Dajie
• Map M2 • 8403 3500 • Subway: Dong Si Shi Tiao • Open 9am–5pm daily; last entry 4pm • Audio guides ¥10 (plus ¥100 deposit) • www.namoc.org

10 Zhong Shan Park

Northwest of the Tian'an Men, Zong Shan (also known as Sun Yat Sen Park) offers respite from the crowds thronging the nearby sights. The park was once part of the grounds of a temple and the square Altar of Earth and Harvests remains. In the eastern section is the Forbidden City Concert Hall, Beijing's premier venue for classical music.
✎ Map L4 • 6605 5431 • Subway: Tian'an Men West • Open 6am–9pm daily • ¥3
• www.zhongshan-park.cn

A Day Around Tian'an Men Square and Wangfujing Dajie

Morning

🕐 Arrive early to beat the crowds at **Mao's Mausoleum** (see p14) and shuffle through for the permitted few minutes in the presence of the Great Helmsman. The Forbidden City can be saved for another day, but climb the **Tian'an Men** (see p14) for the views from the gallery. From the gate, walk east along the Imperial City wall, soon arriving at an entrance overlooked by most visitors: this leads to the **Imperial Ancestral Temple**, once one of the city's most important places of worship. Carry on east after the junction with Nan Chizi, cutting back inside the wall to walk through pleasant **Changpu He Park**. One (long) block beyond the park is Wangfujing Dajie and the Oriental Plaza mall, with a superb **food court** in the basement.

Afternoon

🕐 Wander up **Wangfujing Dajie**, making sure to look in the chopstick and tea shops. At No. 74 is the attractive **St. Joseph's Church**, which is well worth a look. Immediately before the church is a crossroads: head away from the church along Deng Shi Kou Jie looking for signs for Fengfu Hutong on your right. Here is the **Former Residence of Writer Lao She**, offering a glimpse into a way of life fast disappearing in Beijing. Retrace your steps down Wangfujing to Dong'an Men Dajie where the famous **Night Market** should by now be set up.

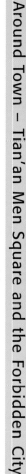

Left **Oriental Plaza** Center **Ten Fu's Tea** Right **Foreign Languages Bookstore**

🔟 Shops, Malls, and Markets

1 Oriental Plaza
Several floors of big-name international high-end retailers, from Apple and Sony to Armani and Paul Smith. Don't expect any bargains. ◈ *1 Dong Chang'an Jie • Map N5*

2 Foreign Languages Bookstore
Most of the ground floor here is devoted to English-language fiction and non-fiction works. Staff are reliably surly. ◈ *235 Wangfujing Dajie • Map N4*

3 Ten Fu's Tea
Tea from all over China, sold loose or in beautiful presentation boxes. Staff will even brew small cups for sampling. ◈ *88 Wangfujing Dajie • Map N4 • www.tenfu.com*

4 APM
This shopping mall full of mid-range clothes shops also has a multiscreen cinema and lots of restaurants up on the top floor. ◈ *138 Wangfujing Dajie • Map N4*

5 Beijing Arts & Crafts Central Store
A vast, multi-story emporium of all kinds of Chinese handicrafts, from cloisonné vases and jade, to wood-carvings, lacquer ware, and silks. ◈ *200 Wangfujing Dajie • Map N4*

6 Mao's Mausoleum
The mausoleum gift shop is the best source of Mao badges, posters, and shoulder bags. ◈ *Tian'an Men Square • Map L5 • Subway: Qian Men • Open 8:30–11:30am Mon–Sat, 2–4pm Mon, Wed & Fri*

7 Hong Cao Wan'r
An upmarket ladies' clothing boutique, Hong Cao Wan'r specializes in designer oriental items in natural fabrics. ◈ *28 Wangfujing Dajie • Map N3 • Subway: Dengshikou*

8 Intime Lotte
This high-end mall sells many Korean brands, which is not surprising, since it is jointly owned by the Korean department giant Lotte and the Chinese Intime group. Cultural events and exhibitions are also held here. ◈ *88 Wangfujing Dajie • Map N4*

9 Jun Yi Home
Chinese military surplus store with badges, patches, and even uniforms. ◈ *383 Dong Si Bei Dajie • Map N2 • Subway: Dong Si*

10 Hao Yuan Market
Small street market just off Wangfujing, which is crammed with stalls selling all kinds of knick-knacks, handicrafts, and curios. ◈ *Off Wangfujing Dajie • Map N4*

70

Price Categories

For the equivalent of a meal for two made up of a range of dishes, served with tea, and including service.

¥ under ¥100
¥¥ ¥100–¥250
¥¥¥ ¥250–¥500
¥¥¥¥ over ¥500

Above **Wangfujing Night Market**

TOP 10 Restaurants

1 Wangfujing Night Market
A line-up of 40 or 50 stalls entice and repulse in equal measure with meat kebabs but also flame-grilled snake and scorpions. ◊ *Dong'an Men Dajie • Map M4 • Open from 5.30pm daily • Y*

2 Oriental Plaza Food Court
The basement of this upscale shopping mall has a Southeast Asian-style food court offering everything from Chinese street foods to sushi. ◊ *Corner of Dong Chang'an Jie and Wangfujing Dajie • Map N4 • ¥*

3 Quanjude
Beijing's most famous duck restaurant has several branches but this is the most convenient, just a few steps off southern Wangfujing. ◊ *9 Shuai Fu Yuan Hutong, Wangfujing Dajie • Map N5 • 6525 3310 • Closes at 9pm • ¥¥*

4 Huang Ting
Enjoy Cantonese cuisine amid splendid antique furniture in the basement of a five-star hotel *(see p59)*. ◊ *The Peninsula Beijing Hotel, 8 Jinyu Hutong • Map N4 • 6510 6707 • ¥¥¥*

5 Made In China
Classy venture with stunning design and even better food *(see p58)*. ◊ *Grand Hyatt, 1 Dong Chang'an Jie • Map N5 • 6510 9608 • ¥¥¥*

6 My Humble House
High-concept fusion food is served in a beautiful conservatory-like setting next door to the Grand Hyatt. ◊ *W3 West Tower, Oriental Plaza, 1 Dong Chang'an Jie • Map N5 • 8518 8811 • ¥¥¥*

7 Princess Mansion
Refined imperial court cuisine in a mansion that once belonged to the Empress Cixi. Excellent food comes with theatrical frills. ◊ *9 Daqudeng Hutong, off Meishuguan Hou Dajie • Map N1 • 6407 8006 • ¥¥¥*

8 CourtYard
One of Beijing's most famous restaurants – lauded as much for its location as for the food. ◊ *95 Donghua Men Dajie • Map M4 • 6526 8883 • Open 6–10pm daily • ¥¥¥¥*

9 Jing
Jing offers an outstanding Asian-flavored fusion menu in refined surrounds *(see p61)*. ◊ *The Peninsula Beijing Hotel, 8 Jinyu Hutong • Map N4 • 6510 6714 • Open 5:30–11:30pm daily • ¥¥¥¥*

10 Tiandi
Classic imperial cuisine in a glamorous setting just steps from the Forbidden City. ◊ *40 Nanchizi Dajie • Map M5 • 8511 5556 • ¥¥¥*

Left **Natural History Museum** Right **Liulichang Jie**

South of Tian'an Men Square

THE QIAN MEN (FRONT GATE) at the southern end of Tian'an Men Square was once part of the inner city walls. These divided the imperial quarters of the Manchu emperors from the "Chinese city," where the massed populace lived apart from their overlords. Walking south from the gate you are immediately plunged into a network of narrow and lively hutongs (alleys), the remnants of the old quarter. Continuing south down Qian Men Dajie eventually brings you to the western perimeter of the grounds of the Temple of Heaven, one of Beijing's most evocative sights.

Imperial Vault of Heaven

Sights

1. Urban Planning Museum
2. Qian Men and Dazhalan
3. Liulichang
4. Legation Quarter
5. Temple of Heaven
6. Natural History Museum
7. Ancient Architecture Museum
8. Cow Street Mosque
9. Fayuan Temple
10. South Cathedral

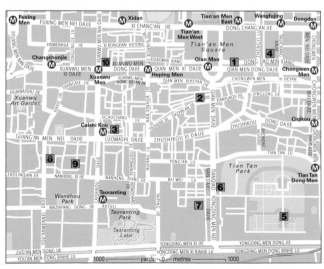

Urban Planning Museum

1 On display at this four-floor museum are dreams of the architecture and urban landscape of Beijing to be. These are dramatically represented through the medium of film and inter-active exhibits, plus a vast model that covers most of the third floor. An interesting section is dedicated to Beijing's comprehensive urban makeover for the 2008 Olympics. ✆ 20 Qian Mon Dong Dajie • Map L6 • 6701 7074 • Subway: Qian Mon • Open 9am–5pm Tue–Sun • ¥30 • www.bjghzl.com.cn

Qian Men and Dazhalan

2 A historical royal street and traditional shopping area, Qian Men Dajie has been redeveloped into a period-themed shopping boulevard replete with a faux-1920s tram and birdcage-like streetlamps. Running west off the northern end of Qian Men is Dazhalan Jie (also known as Dashilan), an old *hutong* area that is great for exploring on foot or by rickshaw. It is full of Qing era specialty shops selling pickles, tea, silks, and traditional Chinese medicine. ✆ Map D5–E5 • Subway: Qian Men

Liulichang

3 Head west from the bustle of Qian Men and Dazhalan into a more peaceful *hutong* district. Historically a gathering spot for

Dazhalan Jie

Beijing Police Museum, Legation Quarter

writers, artists, and musicians, Liulichang takes its name from the imperial glazed tile factory once located here. The streets are lined with shops selling Chinese paintings, musical instruments, porcelain, and calligraphy – look out for the giant ink brushes hanging in the windows. During Chinese New Year, Liulichang is home to one of Beijing's most colorful and traditional Temple Fairs. ✆ Map D5 • Subway: Caishi Kou

Legation Quarter

4 At the end of the Second Opium War, in 1860, foreign delegations were permitted to take up residence in a quarter southeast of the Forbidden City. On main Dong Jiao Min Xiang and surrounding streets, the first modern foreign buildings in Beijing took root. The embassies have long since left, and new occupants have moved in. The former American legation, for instance, is now a restaurant, bar, and lifestyle complex. Also here are the former City Bank of New York, now the Beijing Police Museum *(see p43)*, and St. Michael's Church *(see p47)*. ✆ Map M5 • Subway: Qian Men

Temple of Heaven

to skip the partially dissected human cadavers, also pickled in formaldehyde, which are displayed up on the third floor. ✆ *126 Tangqiao Nan Dajie • Map E6 • 6702 7702 • Subway: Qian Men, then bus 15 • Open 9am–4pm daily • www.bmnh.org.cn*

Ancient Architecture Museum

Housed in the Hall of Jupiter, part of the Xiannong Tan temple complex, this museum offers an excellent introduction to the ancient construction techniques of Beijing buildings, all helpfully illuminated with detailed models. A fascinating three-dimensional plan shows the city as it was in 1949, its city walls and gates largely intact. ✆ *21 Dongjing Lu • Map D6 • 6304 5608 • Bus 15 to Nanwei Lu • Open 9am–4pm Tue–Sun • ¥10*

Cow Street Mosque (Niu Jie)

Beijing's oldest and largest mosque dates back to the 10th century. It's an attractive building with Islamic motifs and Arabic verses decorating its halls and assorted stelae. Astronomical observations were made from the tower-like Wangyue Lou. The courtyard is lush with greenery, making it an idyllic escape from the city streets. Visitors should dress conservatively, and non-Muslims are not allowed to enter the prayer hall. ✆ *88 Niu Jie • Map C6 • 6353 2564 • Subway: Xuanwu Men, then bus • Open 8am–sunset daily • ¥10*

Temple of Heaven

The name refers to a vast complex that encompasses a large, marble sacrificial altar, the iconic three-story Hall of Prayer for Good Harvests, the smaller Imperial Vault of Heaven, and many ancillary buildings, all set in a landscaped park. Allow at least a half day to take in everything *(see pp12–13)*.

Natural History Museum

An overbearing piece of 1950s architecture houses a great collection of dinosaur skeletons, as well as stuffed pandas and other animals. There are also fish, both dead (preserved in formaldehyde) and alive (in the aquarium). Visitors of a nervous disposition may want

---

The Boxers

The Boxers, a band of xenophobic rebels from north China who rose up to rid China of the "foreign devils," drew from superstitious rituals that they believed had made them invulnerable. Supported by the Empress Dowager Cixi, the rebels laid waste to Beijing's Legation Quarter in 1900 while besieging the district's foreign population. The siege was eventually broken by an eight-power allied force.

Cow Street Mosque

South Cathedral

Fayuan Temple

9 This temple dates back to AD 696 and is probably the oldest temple in Beijing. All this time later, it remains a hive of activity. The layout is typical of Buddhist temples. Near the gate, the incense burner is flanked by the Drum and Bell Towers to the east and west. Beyond, the Hall of the Heavenly Kings is guarded by a pair of bronze lions. The Scripture Hall at the temple's rear stores *sutras*, while another hall contains a 16-ft (5-m) statue of Buddha.
⊗ *7 Fayuan Si Qian Jie • Map C6 • 6353 4171 • Subway: Xuanwu Men, then bus • Open 8:30am–3:30pm daily • ¥5*

South Cathedral

10 The first Catholic church to be built in Beijing stands on the site of the residence of the first Jesuit missionary to reach the city, Matteo Ricci. Arriving in 1601, the Italian won the favor of the Wanli emperor by presenting him with gifts of European curiosities such as clocks and mathematical instruments. Ricci founded the church in 1605, although the present building dates to 1904, replacing a structure that was burned down during the Boxer Rebellion. It boasts some fine stained-glass windows. ⊗ *141 Qian Men Xi Dajie • Map J6 • Subway: Xuanwu Men*

A Day South of Tian'an Men Square

Morning

🕐 Start on Tian'an Men Square, at the southeast corner beside the stripey brick **Old Qian Men Railway Station**, built by the British in 1901, partly to bring military forces straight to the assistance of foreigners in the event of a repeat of the siege of the Boxers *(see p71)*. It's now a shopping mall and Beijing Opera theater. Venture east along Dong Jiao Min Xiang into the **Foreign Legation** to visit the **Police Museum** *(see p43)*. On leaving, head south to main Qian Men Dong Dajie and walk back west for a glimpse of the Beijing of the future at the **Urban Planning Museum**.

🗺 From the museum, it is a short walk south into the *hutongs* for a fowl lunch at the legendary **Liqun Roast Duck Restaurant** *(see p77)*.

Afternoon

After eating, if you walk south you'll hit main Xianyukou Jie, which, followed west, becomes **Dazhalan Jie**. This is a great place for specialty shops. Located down the first alley on the left is century-old **Liubiju**, selling a vast array of pickles. **Ruifuxiang**, on the north side of Dazhalan, dates from 1893 and is renowned for silks. **Tongrentang Pharmacy** has been in business since 1669, while **Zhangyiyuan Chazhuang** has been trading teas since the early 20th century. At the end of Dazhalan, head north up Nan Xinhua Jie to the **Ji Gu Ge Teahouse**, to sample more teas in an atmospheric setting.

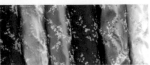

Left **Hong Qiao Market** Right **Beijing Silk Store**

🔟 Shops

1 Hong Qiao Market
Specializing in pearls and precious stones, this vast indoor market also sells clothes, bags, and shoes *(see p50)*. 🔊 *36 Hong Qiao Lu • Map F6 • Open 10am–7pm daily*

2 Liulichang
Picturesque street renovated in the 1980s to give it that Old China look, but still fun to browse for antiques and art supplies *(see p73)*.

3 Tongrentang Pharmacy
Founded in 1669, Tongrentang is China's oldest pharmacy. The store stocks thousands of traditional medicines, some of which were used in the imperial court. 🔊 *24 Qian Men Dazhalan • Map E5*

4 Ruifuxiang
Silk has been sold on this precise spot since 1893. Tailors can make blouses and *qipaos* (the old-style Chinese dress). 🔊 *5 Dazhalan Xijie, off Qian Men Dajie • Map E5 • 6303 5313 • Open 9am–9pm daily*

5 Panjiayuan Antique Market
Set the alarm for dawn for a treasure hunt down at Beijing's sprawling flea market, where anything and everything turns up eventually *(see p50)*. 🔊 *Panjiayuan Qiao • Map H6 • 6775 2405 • Subway: Jinsong • Open 8:30am–6pm Mon–Fri, 4:30am–6pm Sat, Sun*

6 Beijing Curio City
Just south of Panjiayuan, Curio City has four levels packed with antiques, porcelain, carpets, Buddhist statues, jewelry, and furniture. 🔊 *21 Dong San Huan Nan Lu • Map H6 • 6774 7711 • Subway: Jinsong • Open 10am–7pm daily*

7 Neiliansheng
Beijing's best known shoe store, in business since 1853. Infamous for supplying footwear to Chairman Mao. 🔊 *34 Dazhalan Jie • Map E5 • 6301 4863*

8 Beijing Silk Store
Venerable store said to date back to 1840. Prices for quality tailoring, ready-made clothes, and fine cloths are reasonable. 🔊 *Zhubao Shi 5 • Map L6 • 6301 6658*

9 Yuanlong Silk Company
Hugely popular multi-story emporium specializing in all things silken. 🔊 *15 Yongding Men Dong Jie • Map E6 • 6702 2288*

10 Liubiju
A jar of Chinese pickles may not be high on your list of essentials, but a visit to this colorful, 400-year-old shop should be. 🔊 *3 Liangshidian Jie • Map E5*

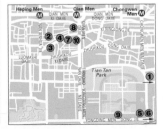

Most shops, markets, and malls tend to be open approximately 9am–9pm daily. For shopping tips **See p111**

Price Categories

For the equivalent of a meal for two made up of a range of dishes, served with tea, and including service.

¥	under ¥100
¥¥	¥100–¥250
¥¥¥	¥250–¥500
¥¥¥¥	over ¥500

Lao She Teahouse

 Restaurants and Teahouses

1 Duyichu
Centuries-old corner snack shop serving *baozi* (steamed buns). *36 Qian Men Dajie • Map L6 • 6702 1555 • ¥*

2 Lao Beijing Zhajiang Mian Da Wang
A bustling eatery selling traditional Beijing snacks. Kitsch but cheap and very tasty fare. *29 Chongwen Men Wai Dajie • Map N6 • 6705 6705 • ¥*

3 Lost Heaven
A luxuriously designed restaurant serving a tangy fusion of Yunnan, Thai, and Burmese cuisines. *23 Chien Men Qian Men Dong Dajie• Map E4 • 8516 2698 • ¥¥¥*

4 Liqun Roast Duck Restaurant
Beijing duck at this chaotic little courtyard restaurant is usually sublime, despite the rough-and-ready ambience. *11 Beixianteng Hutong, enter from Zhengyi Lu • Map M6 • 6705 5578 • ¥¥*

5 Qian Men Quanjude
The most famous of the Quanjude restaurants and the worse for it. But call by for take-away duck pancakes. *32 Qian Men Dajie • Map L6 • 6511 2418 • ¥¥*

6 Gongdelin Vegetarian Restaurant
Guaranteed meat free, although many dishes feature "mock meat," which can look like the real thing. *2 Qian Men Dong Dajie • Map E5 • 6702 0867 • ¥*

7 Capital M
Truly innovative international cuisine proves more than equal to the splendid view across Tian'an Men Square at Australian restaurateur Michelle Garnault's Beijing outpost *3/F, 2 Qian Men Dajie • Map L6 • 6702 2727 • ¥¥¥¥*

8 Lao She Teahouse
One of the first in a renaissance of old-style Beijing teahouses. Performances of opera and acrobatics take place in a small upstairs theater. *3 Qian Men Xi Dajie • Map L6 • 6303 6830 • www.laosheteahouse.com*

9 Ji Gu Ge Teahouse
In addition to tea in all its many kinds and a variety of snacks, the Ji Gu Ge also boasts a small gallery and shop. *132–6 Liulichang Dong Jie • Map K6 • 6301 7849*

10 Maison Boulud
The Beijing outpost of chef Daniel Boulud serves exquisite French cuisine in the stately setting of the former American embassy. *32 Qian Men Dong Dajie • Map M6 • 6559 9200 • ¥¥¥¥*

Unless otherwise stated, all restaurants are open for lunch and dinner. Only top-end places accept credit cards

77

Left **Hou Hai bars** Center **Qian Hai** Right **Bell Tower**

North of the Forbidden City

B Y FAR THE MOST REWARDING AREA *to explore on foot, north of the Forbidden City stretches an almost contiguous run of lakes, either set in parkland or surrounded by swathes of charming historic hutongs. It's an area rich in temple architecture and dotted with grand old courtyard residences. Its appeal to visitors has resulted in restaurants, bars, and shops flooding in to take advantage of the picturesque settings, but thankfully much of the growth has so far been sympathetic.*

Mahjong players at Hou Hai

🔟 Sights

1. Bei Hai Park
2. Hou Hai
3. Drum Tower
4. Bell Tower
5. Nan Luogu Xiang
6. Xu Beihong Memorial Museum
7. Former Residence of Mei Lanfang
8. Lama Temple
9. Confucius Temple
10. Di Tan Park

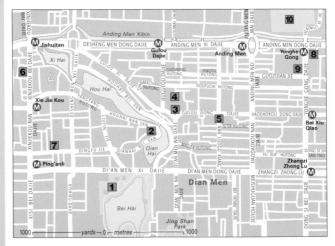

➡ *Rickshaws cluster mainly around Qian Hai offering tours around the lakes and hutongs. It's a fine way to see the are©ip21*

Bei Hai Park

Hou Hai

The most visitor-friendly neighborhood of Beijing, Hou Hai consists of three joined lakes surrounded by an expansive and labyrinthine sprawl of age-old *hutongs* (alleys). Visit for a handful of well-preserved mansions, as well as the opportunity to see a more humble form of Beijing life as it has been lived for centuries *(see pp20–21)*.

Bei Hai Park

A beautiful example of a classic imperial garden, Bei Hai was a summer playground for successive dynasties that ruled from the neighboring Forbidden City. Today, it is well and truly open to the public, and thronged daily by locals who come here to socialize. There are a couple of small temples, a fine, small ornamental garden, and a noted restaurant. This is arguably the most lovely of Beijing's many fine city parks *(see pp18–19)*.

Drum Tower

Drum towers *(gu lou)* were once found in all major Chinese towns. They housed large drums that were beaten to mark the hour, keeping the city's civil servants on time for work. There has been such a tower on this site since 1272, although the current structure dates to 1420. Visitors can clamber up the torturously steep steps to inspect some 25 drums and be entertained by a troop of drummers that delivers skin thumping performances on the hour.
- Gulou Dong Dajie • Map E2
- 8403 6706 • Subway: Gulou Dajie
- Open 9am–5:30pm daily • ¥20

An exercise park beside Hou Hai

Confucius

Born in Shandong Province, south of Beijing, during an age of uninterrupted war, Confucius (551–479 BC) was prompted by the suffering around him to develop a practical philosophy built on the principle of virtue. Finding no audience among his native rulers, he embarked on a journey in search of a ruler who would apply his rules of governance. He never found such a person and died unrecognized.

Bell Tower

This dates from 1745 and replaces an earlier tower that burnt down. The great 42-ton (42,674-kg) bell it contains used to be rung to mark the closing of the city gates in the evening. During Spring Festival visitors are allowed to ring the bell for a donation of ¥100. The views from both the Drum and Bell Towers over the neighboring *hutongs* are well worth the exhausting climb. ◈ *Gulou Dong Dajie • Map E1 • 8403 6706 • Subway: Gulou Dajie • Open 9am–5:30pm daily • ¥15*

Nan Luogu Xiang

Less than 10 minutes' walk east of the Drum Tower, Nan Luogu Xiang is arguably Beijing's hippest *hutong*. Still traditional in feel, the alley is home to quite a few small hotels, as well as several interesting clothing and craft boutiques, and an ever-increasing number of cafés and bars. The nearby Baochao Hutong is an up-and-coming hipster hangout. ◈ *Map E2*

Xu Beihong Memorial Museum

Set back from the road with a sign on top in green characters, this museum is dedicated to the man regarded as the founder of modern Chinese painting. It exhibits a collection of the lively watercolors of horses that made Xu Beihong (1885–1953) internationally famous. ◈ *53 Xinjiekou Bei Dajie • Map D1 • 6225 2187 • Subway: Jishuitan • Open 9am–4pm Tue–Sun • ¥10 (audio guide ¥10, plus ¥100 deposit)*

Former Residence of Mei Lanfang

This was the home of Beijing Opera's greatest ever performer (1894–1961). The rear rooms have been left with their traditional furniture as it was when he died. Others contain a hagiographic account of his life, as well as diagrams of the stylized movements required by the form and a video of Mei, already 61, but still playing the young girl roles for which he was famous *(see p39)*. ◈ *9 Huguosi Jie • Map D2 • 8322 3598 • Subway: Jishuitan • Open 9am–4pm Tue–Sun • ¥10 • www.meilanfang.com.cn*

Lama Temple (Yonghegong)

About a 30-minute walk east of the Drum and Bell Towers, or just a few minutes south of the

Lama Temple

Di Tan Park

Yonghe Gong subway station, the Lama Temple is Beijing's largest working temple complex. It is filled every day with about an equal number of worshipers and visitors *(see pp16–17)*.

9 Confucius Temple (Kong Miao)

Just west of the Lama Temple, the Confucius Temple was built in 1302 during the Mongol Yuan dynasty, and expanded in 1906. Around 200 ancient stelae stand in the courtyard in front of the main hall, inscribed with the names of those who successfully passed the imperial civil service exams. On a marble terrace inside the hall are statues of Confucius and some of his disciples. ◈ *13 Guozijian Jie • Map F1 • 8402 7224 • Subway: Yonghe Gong • Open 8:30am–4:30pm daily • ¥20*

10 Di Tan Park

The park was named after the Temple of Earth (Di Tan), which was a venue for imperial sacrifices. The altar's square shape represents the earth. These days, the park is always full of pensioners strolling, chatting, and exercising. A lively temple fair is held here at Chinese New Year. ◈ *North of Lama Temple • Map F1 • 6421 4657 • Subway: Yonghe Gong • Open 6am–9pm daily • Park ¥2; Altar ¥5 • www.dtpark.com*

A Day in the Hutongs

Morning

🕐 Take an early morning stroll along **Wudingyao Hutong**, where you can have breakfast at one of the cafés. Then continue on to the **Lama Temple**. On leaving, cross over the main road and pass under the *pailou* (gate) at the entrance to Guozijian Jie for the **Confucius Temple**. Afterwards, take a break at the lovely **Confucius Teahouse** *(see p59)* over the road. At the western end of Guozijian Jie turn left onto Anding Men Nei Dajie, a wide, shop-filled avenue, then follow it south across Jiaodaokuo Dong Dajie and take the first right into **Ju'er Hutong**, one of the most vibrant of the city's old alleys. Take the first left onto **Nan Luogu Xiang**, and stop for lunch at one of the many cafés.

Afternoon

Head west along **Mao'er Hutong** until you reach main **Di'an Men Wai Dajie**, where you turn right and head up the street for the splendid **Drum and Bell Towers**. Climb the towers to pick out the route you've just taken. Retrace your steps back down Di'an Men Wai Dajie taking the very first right, a tiny opening (usually marked by waiting taxis) leading into bustling **Yandai Xie Jie**. At the end of this crooked alley is the **Silver Ingot Bridge**; cross and bear left for **Lotus Lane**. You can stop here for coffee or head round the southern tip of the lake to **Han Cang** *(see p83)* for a terrific meal of Hakka cuisine.

Left **Mai** Right **Fu Family Teahouse**

Bars and Teahouses

1 Bed Tapas & Bar
A short walk north of the Drum and Bell Towers, Bed makes the absolute most of its old courtyard house setting *(see p62)*. ◎ *17 Zhang Wang Hutong, off Jiu Gulou Dajie • Map E1 • 8400 1554*

2 Modernista
Keep the winter chill at bay with the delicious warm wine served at this 1920s-themed jazz and piano bar. In summer, try their sangria *(see p63)*. ◎ *44 Baochao Hutong • Map E1 • 136 7127 4747*

3 Lotus Bar
Another fine Yandai Xie Jie bar, this one squeezed into a narrow, two-story house with a compact, boho interior and roof terrace. ◎ *29 Yandai Xie Jie • Map E2 • 6407 7857*

4 Zajia
Located near the Bell Tower, this cozy bar has a cool vibe, and is popular with the local media and fashion set. ◎ *21 Doufuchi Hutong • Map E2 • 6407 6778*

5 Contempio
Sip cocktails at this suave lounge and patio bar housed in an old temple. The garden with a fountain is very peaceful. ◎ *23 Doufuchi Hutong • Map E2 • 8404 9141*

6 No Name Bar
The perfect lakeside drinking den. Expect stiff competition from the house cat for the best seats *(see p62)*. ◎ *3 Qianhai Dongyan • Map E2 • 6401 8541*

7 Mai
Visit this tiny bar to choose from a wide range of cocktails – professionally mixed by a trained mixologist *(see p62)*. ◎ *40 Beiluogu Xiang • Map E1 • 138 1125 2641*

8 East Shore Live Jazz Café
Opened by legendary jazzman Liu Yuan. Climb steep wooden stairs to four walls of floor-to-ceiling windows and a roof terrace, plus live music. ◎ *2 Qianhai Nanyan Lu • Map E2 • 8403 2131*

9 The Orchid Bar
A cool rooftop bar that sits atop a renovated *siheyuan* courtyard home, this is a great spot to sip a sundowner cocktail. Enjoy views over the low-rise *hutongs* towards the Drum Tower. ◎ *65 Baochao Hutong • Map E1 • 8404 4818*

10 Fu Family Teahouse
Modeled after a Qing-era home, this teahouse is filled with antique furniture and often has live Chinese music. ◎ *Hou Hai Nan Yan • Map E2 • 8328 6313*

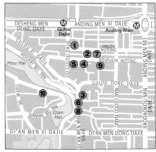

Unless otherwise stated bars are generally open from around noon until 2am

Price Categories

For the equivalent of a meal for two made up of a range of dishes, served with tea, and including service.

¥ under ¥100
¥¥ ¥100–¥250
¥¥¥ ¥250–¥500
¥¥¥¥ over ¥500

Left **Han Cang** Center **Raj**

TOP 10 Restaurants

1 Dali Courtyard
Book ahead for the spicy Yunnan dishes at this laid-back restaurant in a beautiful courtyard. ◈ 67 Xiaojingchang Hutong, Gulou Dong Dajie • Map E2 • 8404 1430 • ¥¥

2 Cafe Sambal
An old-style courtyard house serves as the venue for exquisite dishes prepared by an authentic Malaysian chef (see p60). ◈ 43 Doufuchi Hutong, off Jiu Gulou Dajie • Map E1 • 6400 4875 • ¥¥

3 Han Cang
Bustling two-story rustic restaurant with a large outdoor dining area always packed with locals enjoying simple, tasty Hakka dishes. ◈ Ping'an Dadao • Map E2 • 6404 2259 • ¥¥

4 Kaorou Ji
Majors in Qingzhen – Hui or Muslim – cuisine, which means mutton. The house specialty is spiced barbecued lamb and sesame seed bread. ◈ 14 Qianhai Dong Yan • Map E2 • 6404 2554 • ¥¥

5 Kong Yiji
Lakeside restaurant with a range of exquisite dishes from the Yangzi River delta. ◈ Desheng Men Nei Dajie • Map E2 • 6618 4917 • ¥¥

6 Nuage
Well-respected Vietnamese with a lovely location just south of the Silver Ingot Bridge (see p61). ◈ 22 Qian Hai Dong Yan • Map E2 • 6401 9581 • ¥¥

7 Raj
Cheap and authentic south Indian cuisine. The decor is kitsch but there's a pleasant rooftop terrace. ◈ 31 Gulou Xidajie • Map F1 • 6401 1675 • ¥¥

8 Southern Barbarian
The menu at this upmarket eatery offers classic Yunnan dishes, as well as a wide selection of international beers. ◈ 107 Baochao Hutong • Map E1–2 • 6401 3318 • ¥¥¥

9 Mei Fu (Mei Mansion)
The setting is a gorgeous courtyard house lavishly filled with antiques. Set menus of sweet and rich Shanghainese cuisine start from ¥200 per person. ◈ 24 Daxiangfeng Hutong • Map D2 • 6612 6847 • ¥¥¥

10 Li Family Imperial Cuisine
Intimate courtyard restaurant serving imperial court cuisine. Set menus range from ¥200 to ¥1,500 a head but the food is exquisite. ◈ 11 Yangfang Hutong • Map D2 • 6618 0107 • ¥¥¥–¥¥¥¥

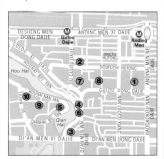

Unless otherwise stated, all restaurants are open for lunch and dinner. Only top-end places accept credit cards

83

Left **Sanlitun bar** Right **Red Gate Gallery at the Southeast Corner Watchtower**

Eastern Beijing

EAST OF CENTRAL BEIJING, *in a corridor between the Second and Third Ring Roads, is the district of Chaoyang. It's not an area that is particularly old and it doesn't have very many significant monuments, but it is home to two main clusters of international embassies, and it is where a large proportion of the city's foreign expatriate community chooses to live. As a result, Chaoyang is the city's entertainment and nightlife center, and, for the visitor, it is the prime area for eating and shopping.*

🔟 Sights

1. Ancient Observatory
2. Southeast Corner Watchtower
3. Ri Tan Park
4. Central Business District (CBD)
5. Dong Yue Miao
6. Blue Zoo Beijing
7. Workers' Stadium
8. Sanlitun
9. Ghost Street
10. Lufthansa Center

Crowds at the Workers' Stadium

Ri Tan Park

Distances in eastern Beijing are considerable and it may be preferable to take taxis between some of the sights

Ancient Observatory

Ancient Observatory

Dating to 1442, Beijing's observatory is one of the oldest in the world. In fact, there was an even earlier Yuan-dynasty (1279–1368) observatory also located on this site but no trace of that remains. Today, a collection of reproduction astronomical devices lies in the courtyard, some decorated with fantastic Chinese designs. There are more impressive instruments on the roof. ✆ *Map G4 • 6524 2202 • Subway: Jianguo Men • Open 9am–4pm daily • ¥10*

Southeast Corner Watchtower

A short walk south of the Second Ring Road an imposing chunk of the old Beijing city wall survives, including the 15th-century Dong Bian Men watchtower. Visitors can climb onto the battlements and walk along a stretch of wall. The tower is also home to Red Gate Gallery, one of Beijing's best contemporary art venues *(see p49)*. ✆ *South of Jianguo Men Nei Dajie • Map G5 • 8512 1554 • Subway: Jianguo Men • Open 8am–5:30pm daily • ¥10*

Ri Tan Park

One of the city's oldest parks, Ri Tan was laid out around a sacrificial altar back in the 16th century. The round altar remains, ringed by a circular wall, but this is very much a living park, filled daily with people walking and exercising. Being at the heart of the embassy district, the park is well tended and surrounded by lots of good restaurants and cafés. ✆ *Guanghua Lu • Map G1 • 8561 6301 • Subway: Jianguo Men • Open 6:30am–9:30pm daily*

Central Business District (CBD)

The Central Business District is Beijing's business hub, housing more than 60 percent of the city's foreign-funded companies. Marked by the CCTV Tower in the northwest and by the Twin Towers of the China World Trade Center in the southeast, the area is also home to about half of the city's luxury hotels and two of its glitziest shopping malls, China World and Shin Kong Plaza *(see p51 and p88)*. ✆ *Map H4 • Subway: Guomao or Dawanglu*

Southeast Corner Watchtower

 *For more modern architecture in eastern Beijing **See pp40–41***

Dong Yue Miao

This colorful and active temple, dating to the early 14th century, was restored in 1999 and is tended by Daoist monks. The main courtyard leads into the Hall of Tai Shan with statues of gods and their attendants. Tai Shan is another name for Dong Yue, in Daoist lore the Eastern peak to which the spirits of the dead travel.
ⓢ *141 Chaoyang Men Wai Dajie • Map G3 • 6551 0151 • Subway: Chaoyang Men • Open 8:30am–4:30pm Tue–Sun • ¥10*

Dong Yue Miao

Blue Zoo Beijing

Not a zoo at all, but an excellent modern aquarium, reckoned to be the best of its kind in Asia. The main attraction is a central tank holding literally thousands of fish, plus there are also 18 additional tanks with specifically themed displays (*see p53*). ⓢ *South gate of Workers' Stadium • Map G3 • 6591 3397 • Subway: Chaoyang Men • Open 8:30am–7:30pm daily • ¥75; children ¥50; under 3 ft (1 m) free • www. bluezoo.com.cn*

Workers' Stadium

With an estimated capacity of 72,000, the stadium is home to Beijing's premier football club, Hyundai Guo'an, and it is the city's main venue for large-scale rock and pop concerts. Perplexingly, it's also a hub of Beijing nightlife, with numerous clubs and bars clustered around its north and west gates, and some very good restaurants too (*see p89*). Even oldies get in on the act, with mass open-air dancing taking place on the forecourt of the north gate most summer evenings. ⓢ *Gongren Tiyuchang Bei Lu • Map G2 • 6501 6655 • Subway: Dong Si Shi Tiao*

Sanlitun

Beijing's main expat-friendly shopping, dining, and drinking district is centered around The Village and Nali Patio on Sanlitun Bei Lu, and around Workers' Stadium on Gongren Tiyuchang Bei Lu. It has a high concentration of international restaurants (*see p89*) and lots of boutique

Entrance gate at the Workers' Stadium

Red lanterns lighting up Ghost Street

shopping *(see p88)*, Streets around here, although modern, are tree-lined and, with plenty of cafes for refreshment stops, it's a pleasant district to wander in.
🅂 *Map H2 • Subway: Tuanjiehu*

Ghost Street
Gui Jie, or Ghost Street, is a mile-and-a-quarter (2-km) stretch of Dong Zhi Men Nei Dajie that come nightfall is jammed with cars double-parked outside its one hundred or so restaurants, many of which open 24 hours. The roadside is festively lit with strings of red lanterns bobbing in the breeze, while most establishments favor corny, old-China décor with lots of red lacquer and pagoda motifs, and waitresses in silk tunics. This is the home of hotpot, although all regional Chinese cuisines are represented here. 🅂 *Map F2 • Subway: Beixingqiao*

Lufthansa Center
This glossy mall-style complex caters for aspirational Beijingers with a department store full of imported luxury goods, a basement Continental deli, and a BMW showroom, plus numerous international labels. More down to earth, just west on the south bank of the river is the Liang Ma Flower Market, which is a riot of color and fragrances. 🅂 *50 Liang Ma Qiao Lu • Map H1 • 6465 1188 • Subway: Liangmaqiao • Open 9am–10pm daily*

A Walk From Ri Tan Park to Sanlitun

Morning

🕐 Begin the day with an early morning stroll with the locals through **Ri Tan Park** via the south gate. This is one of the city's best parks, with an old sacrificial altar, a rockery, and a small lake with the waterside **Stone Boat** café. Exit via the west gate onto Ritan Lu, then head south, toward Guanghua Lu, which is lined with shops. Stop at French deli **Fauchon** *(see p88)* to stock up on delicious chocolates and wines, or head to one of the many stores in this area. Continue on to busy Chaoyang Men Wai Dajie and the **Dong Yue Miao** temple finishing at the **Southeast Corner Watchtower** (Dong Bian Men) for a walk on the ancient city wall and a perusal of the art in the Red Gate Gallery.

Afternoon

Departing the Watchtower, catch a cab to the **Workers' Stadium**. Circle the stadium to exit via the north gate onto Gongren Tiyuchang Bei Lu. Head east until you come to a foot bridge, which allows you to cross this eight-lane boulevard safely. It deposits you in front of **Yashow Market** *(see p88)* for more bargain shopping. To the east, **The Village Sanlitun** *(see p88)* offers more up-scale shopping possibilities. On the upper level is the popular Element Fresh café. Wander farther along Sanlitun Bei Lu for some of Beijing's smartest bars and eateries including **Migas** *(see p62)*, **Fez** *(see p63)*, and **Bei** *(see p89)*.

Around Town – Eastern Beijing

Left **Sunglasses at the Silk Market** Center **Boots at Yashow Market** Right **The Village Sanlitun**

Shops, Markets, and Malls

1 Silk Market
This four-story market is the lodestone for counterfeit designer goods. Haggle as if your life depended on it (see p50). ◊ Jianguo Men Wai Dajie • Map G4 • 5169 9003

2 Yashow Market
Although similar to the Silk Market, Yashow (Yaxiu) is much less crowded and less aggressive (see p50). ◊ 58 Gongren Tiyuchang Bei Lu • Map H2 • 6416 8945

3 China World Shopping Mall
The Silk Market and Yashow Market sell the counterfeits, but this is where you come for the originals (see p51). ◊ 1 Jianguo Men Wai Dajie • Map H4 • 6505 2288

4 Shin Kong Plaza
Opened in April 2007, Shin Kong is a temple for luxury shopping and gourmet dining. It marked the debut appearance of many elite brands in mainland China (see p51). ◊ 87 Jianguo Lu • 6530 5888

5 Sanlitun SOHO
Characterized by colorful funnel-shaped buildings, Sanlitun SOHO is a prime example of urban development. It is a vast complex of shopping malls, offices, hotels, and private apartments. Numerous brand stores, banks, cafés, and restaurants occupy the ground floor. ◊ South side of Gongren Tiyuchang Bei Lu • Map H2 • 5878 8888

6 Dong Jiao Wholesale Market
This is where the traders from Beijing's other markets come to buy their stock (see p51). ◊ Dong Si Huan Zhong Lu • Map G4

7 The Place
With its eye-catching overhead LED screen tunnel, The Place is hard to miss. This mall offers mid-range shops like Zara, Aldo, MAC, Crocs, and Puma. There is also an English-language bookshop. ◊ 9 Guanghua Lu • 6587 1188

8 Fauchon
This French gourmet empire opened its first Chinese deli store in Shin Kong Plaza, levels B1–F2. ◊ 87 Jianguo Lu • 6533 1266

9 The Village Sanlitun
The upscale Village has numerous brand stores including Apple and Adidas, plus a range of restaurants and bars. ◊ 6 Gongren Tiyuchang Bei Lu (corner Sanlitun Bei Lu) • Map H2 • 6417 6110

10 Jenny Lou's
Expat heaven with genuine Dutch cheese, German bread, and French wines. ◊ 4 Ri Tan Bei Lu • Map G3 • 8563 0626

Most shops, markets, and malls tend to be open approximately 9am–9pm daily. For shopping tips **See p111**

Price Categories

For the equivalent of a meal for two made up of a range of dishes, served with tea, and including service.

¥	under ¥100
¥¥	¥100–¥250
¥¥¥	¥250–¥500
¥¥¥¥	over ¥500

Above **Hatsune**

🔟 Restaurants

1 Beijing Dadong Roast Duck Restaurant

It is the opinion of a great many Beijingers that there is no finer duck than that served here *(see p58)*. ◎ *Bdg 3, Tuanjiehui Beikou, Dong San Huan • Map I12 • 6582 2892 • ¥¥¥*

2 Bei

A fine-dining venue, Bei has a varied menu inspired by North Asian cuisine. There are good Vegetarian options *(see p60)*. ◎ *1/F The Opposite House Hotel, 11 Sanlitun Bei Lu • Map H2 • 6410 5230 • ¥¥¥¥*

3 Crescent Moon

There are no frills here, just great, exotic food served by a team of friendly Uighur waitresses. Don't miss the tasty lamb kebabs and *dapanji* (chicken and potato stew). ◎ *16 Dong Si Liu Tiao • Map F2 • 6400 5281 • ¥*

4 Bellagio

Packed until the early hours with hip Beijingers filling up on carbs before moving on to one of the clubs up the street *(see p58)*. ◎ *6 Gongren Tiyuchang Xi Lu • Map G2 • 6551 3533 • ¥¥*

5 Guizhou Luo Luo Suan Tang Yu

"Ghost Street" is a fun place to dine, and this hotpot specialist is one of its best eateries. ◎ *186 Dong Zhi Men Nei Dajie • Map F2 • 6405 1717 • ¥¥*

6 Alameda

Beautiful modern restaurant serving Brazilian-inspired contemporary cuisine. ◎ *Na Li Market, off Sanlitun Bei Lu • Map I12 • 6417 8084 • ¥¥¥*

7 Hatsune

A class act: stylish Japanese restaurant with fresh fish flown in daily *(see p60)*. ◎ *2nd floor, Heqiao Building C, 8a Guanghua Dong Lu • Map H4 • 6581 3939 • ¥¥¥*

8 Morel's

Beijing's sole Belgian restaurant is a big expat favorite for steak and seafood, including, of course, mussels, as well as a great range of Belgian beers. ◎ *Gongren Tiyuchang Bei Lu, Chunxiu Lu • Map G2 • 6416 8802 • ¥¥¥*

9 Transit

Enjoy authentic, beautifully spiced Sichuan cuisine at this sophisticated but unpretentious restaurant *(see p58)*. ◎ *N4-36, 3/F The Village North Sanlitun Bei Lu • Map H2 • 6417 9090 • ¥¥¥*

10 Green T. House

Gimmick or culinary wonder? Make your own mind up, but certainly take a look at Beijing's most jaw-dropping, China-meets-Alice-in-Wonderland interior. ◎ *6 Gongren Tiyuchang Xi Lu • Map G2 • 6552 8311 • ¥¥¥¥*

→ *Unless otherwise stated, all restaurants are open for lunch and dinner. Only top-end places accept credit cards*

89

Left **Military Museum of the Chinese People's Revolution** Right **Beijing Aquarium**

Western Beijing

XICHENG, WHICH IN CHINESE MEANS "WEST CITY", *is the central district west of the Forbidden City and the lakes. Beijingers think of this area mostly as a seat of money and learning – both the Financial District and the Haidian University are located here. Western Beijing is best experienced as a series of half-day expeditions: a visit to the Military Museum with a look at the Millennium Monument afterwards and a walk through Yuyuan Tan Park, or a trip to the zoo and aquarium followed by the Temple of the Five Pagodas. Expect to make liberal use of taxis and the subway.*

Temple of the Five Pagodas

Inside the Capital Museum

🔟 Sights

1. Temple of Heavenly Tranquility
2. White Cloud Temple
3. Military Museum of the Chinese People's Revolution
4. Capital Museum
5. Miaoying Temple White Dagoba
6. Lu Xun Museum
7. National Library of China
8. Beijing Zoo
9. Beijing Aquarium
10. Temple of the Five Pagodas

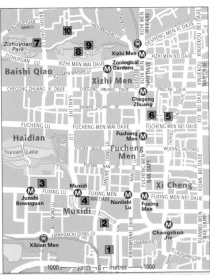

1 Temple of Heavenly Tranquility

Home to Beijing's most striking pagoda, the temple (Tianning Si) was built during the 5th century AD, making it one of the city's oldest. The 196-ft (60-m) octagonal pagoda was added in the early 12th century.

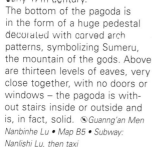
Temple of Heavenly Tranquility

The bottom of the pagoda is in the form of a huge pedestal decorated with carved arch patterns, symbolizing Sumeru, the mountain of the gods. Above are thirteen levels of eaves, very close together, with no doors or windows – the pagoda is without stairs inside or outside and is, in fact, solid. ⊗ Guang'an Men Nanbinhe Lu • Map B5 • Subway: Nanlishi Lu, then taxi

2 White Cloud Temple

The first temple on this site was founded in AD 739 and burnt down in 1166. Since that time, it has been repeatedly destroyed and rebuilt. It even survived being used as a factory during the Cultural Revolution. The shrines, pavilions, and courtyards that make up the compound today date mainly from the Ming and Qing dynasties. Monks here are followers of Daoism and sport distinctive top-knots. Each Chinese New Year this is the venue for one of the city's most popular temple fairs, with performers, artisans, and traders. ⊗ 6 Baiyun Guan Jie, off Lianhuachi Dong Lu • Map B4 • 6340 4812 • Subway: Nanlishi Lu • Open 8:30am–4:30pm daily (Oct 8–Apr: to 4pm) • ¥10

Gateway at the White Cloud Temple

3 Military Museum of the Chinese People's Revolution

Vast halls of Cold War-era hardware, including lots of silvery fighter planes and tanks, fill the ground floor. Upstairs has exhibitions on historic conflicts, including the Opium Wars and Boxer Rebellion. Unfortunately, there is little labeling in English. What is not mentioned is that the museum is close to the Muxidi intersection, scene of a massacre of civilians by the Chinese army during the 1989 democracy protests. ⊗ 9 Fuxing Lu • Map A4 • 6686 6244 • Subway: Junshibowuguan • Open 8am–5pm daily • ¥20 (ID required)

4 Capital Museum

The Capital Museum celebrates China's civilization in general and Beijing's history in particular. The five-story building is easily recognizable thanks to its huge bronze cylinder. Exhibits include porcelain art, calligraphy, Buddha statues, furniture, and crafts. Entrance is free, so the museum is popular. ⊗ 16 Fuxing Men Wai Dajie, Xicheng • Map B4 • 6337 0491 • Subway: Muxidi • Open 9am–5pm Tue–Sun • www.capitalmuseum.org.cn

There are few good restaurants in Western Beijing but Hou Hai, with its excellent dining, is only a short taxi ride away See p83

Buddhism in China

Buddhism, which started in India, probably came to China along the Silk Road. The earliest sign of the religion is associated with the founding of the White Horse Temple near the old capital of Luoyang in AD 68. Buddhism surged in popularity during periods of instability, when Confucianism's veneration for authority did not sit well with the populace. It was eventually adopted by China's rulers.

Miaoying Temple White Dagoba monks

5 Miaoying Temple White Dagoba (Bantaisi)

Celebrated for its Tibetan-styled, 167-ft (51-m) white *dagoba* (stupa), said to have been designed by a Nepalese architect, the temple dates to 1271, when Beijing was under Mongol rule. The temple is also noted for its fascinating collection of thousands of Tibetan Buddhist statues. ◈ *171 Fucheng Men Nei Dajie • Map C3 • 6616 6099 • Subway: Fucheng Men • Open 9am–4pm daily • ¥20*

6 Lu Xun Museum

Lu Xun is regarded as the father of modern Chinese literature, responsible for ground-breaking works such as "Diary of a Madman" and "The True Story of Ah Q". This is the house in which he lived from 1924 to 1926. The rooms display artifacts relating to his life and there's also an adjacent exhibition hall with more than 10,000 letters, journals, photographs, and other personal objects. ◈ *19 Gong Men Kou Er Tiao, off Fucheng Men Nei Dajie • Map C3 • 6616 4168 • Subway: Fucheng Men • Open 9am–3:30pm Tue–Sun • Free*

7 National Library of China

One of the five biggest libraries in the world, the National Library of China has been expanded to accommodate its collection of approximately 12 million books. The building's floating roof houses the Digital Library. Most books are reference only, but visitors can request a reader's pass. ◈ *33 Zhongguancun Nandajie • Map A1 • 8854 5426 • Open 9am–9pm Mon–Fri, 9am–5pm Sat, Sun (except pub hols) • www.nlc.gov.cn*

8 Beijing Zoo

Visit for the pandas, the rare bears that are native to China and nowhere else. The zoo has several, housed in a new "panda house." However, most of the other 2,000 animals here are not so lucky; their cages are tiny. ◈ *137 Xizhi Men Wai Dajie • Map B2 • 6831 5131 • Subway: Xizhi Men • Open 7:30am–6pm daily (till 5pm Nov–Mar) • ¥20 • www.beijingzoo.com*

9 Beijing Aquarium

Located in the northeastern corner of the zoo is this conch shell-shaped building. It's reputedly the largest inland aquarium in the world, with massive tanks containing thousands of weird and wonderful fish, plus a shark tank, coral reefs and an "Amazon rainforest." There are also several dolphin and seal shows held

Beijing Aquarium

daily at 11am and 3pm ◎ 108 Gao Liang Qiao Xijie • Map B2 • 6217 6655 • Open 9am–5pm daily • ¥120 adults, ¥60 children • www.bj-sea.com

🔟 Temple of the Five Pagodas

Just north of the zoo, this temple displays obvious Indian influences. It was built in the early 15th century in honor of an Indian monk who came to China and presented the emperor with five golden Buddhas. The pagodas sport elaborate carvings of curvaceous females, as well as the customary Buddhas. Also here is the Beijing Art Museum of Stone Carvings, with 2,000 decorative stelae. ◎ 24 Wuta Si Cun • Map B1 • 6217 3836 • Subway: Xizhi Men • Open 8:30am–4:30pm daily • ¥15

Temple of the Five Pagodas

War and peace

Morning

🕐 Even if you're no big fan of mechanized heavy armor, the **Military Museum of the Chinese People's Revolution** is a fascinating place. Exhibits begin with the technology that made China one of the world's first military superpowers, including the "Flying Dragon," an early form of missile launcher. There's one room devoted to the wonderfully tacky gifts that have been bestowed on China's army chiefs and leaders, such as a pistol presented to Chairman Mao by Fidel Castro. Mao's limousine is displayed on the ground floor and there's one hall devoted to statues and assorted representations of the Communist Party's great and good. It all makes for a fascinating insight into the mentality of late 20th-century China.

Afternoon

Leaving the museum, walk west along Fuxing Lu and take the first right. You will see the **Millennium Monument** and, behind it, **Yuyuan Tan Park**, with a large lake at its center. The vast park is a relaxing place for a stroll. Afterwards, for some refreshments, walk east to the pleasant **Hong Hao Ge Teahouse** (see p59) before continuing on Fuxing Men Wai Dajie toward Muxidi and the **Capital Museum**. Audio self-guided tours in Chinese and English are available at the entrance. Don't miss the Peking Opera exhibition on the top floor, or the short film on Beijing's urban development, screened in the auditorium on the ground floor.

Left **Marble Boat, Summer Palace** Right **798 Art District**

Greater Beijing

BEIJING IS VAST. *Although you could spend all your time without ever straying too far from the area around central Tian'an Men Square, you would be missing out on a lot. Way out in the northwest of the city is a cluster of sights that includes the unmissable Summer Palace, with the almost equally intoxicating hillside Xiang Shan Park and the haunting ruins of the Yuanming Yuan, or Old Summer Palace, close by. It might be a squeeze to get all three into one day's sightseeing but it's worth a try. For fans of contemporary urban culture, the 798 Art District in the northeast of the city is an absolute must, and you can drop in on the markets and bars around Sanlitun on the way back into town.*

Sights

1. Summer Palace
2. Yuanming Yuan (Old Summer Palace)
3. Xiang Shan Park
4. Great Bell Temple
5. Beijing Botanical Gardens
6. China Ethnic Culture Park
7. Science and Technology Museum
8. China National Film Museum
9. 798 Art District
10. China Railway Museum

Bronze ox, Summer Palace

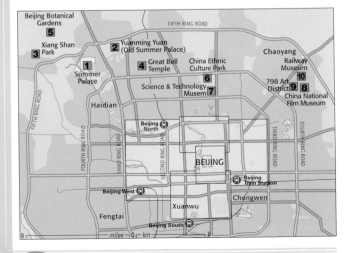

Long Corridor ceiling, Summer Palace

Summer Palace

It's only a short bus or taxi ride from Bagou subway station to the unmissable Summer Palace. The grounds are arranged as a microcosm of nature, with hills and water complemented by bridges, temples and walkways. It manages to be both fanciful and harmonious at the same time (see pp22–3).

Yuanming Yuan (Old Summer Palace)

The name Yuanming Yuan derives from a Buddhist term and can be translated as "Garden of Perfect Brightness". This was the largest and most elaborate of all the summer palaces of the Qing era. It once contained private imperial residences, pleasure pavilions, Buddhist temples, a vast imperial ancestral shrine, pools for goldfish, and canals and lakes for pleasure boating. The Qianlong emperor even added a group of European-style palaces

Guardian deity, Heng

designed by Jesuit missionary-artists serving in the Qing court. Today, all that's left are graceful, fragmentary ruins after the complex was razed to the ground during the Second Opium War (1856–60). A small museum displays images and models of the place as it was.
§ 28 Qinghua Xi Lu • 6262 8501 • Subway: Yuanming Yuan Park • Open 7am–7pm daily • ¥10

Xiang Shan Park

The wooded parkland area, also known as Fragrant Hills Park, is 2 miles (3 km) west of the Summer Palace. It boasts fine views from Incense Burner Peak, which is accessible by a chair lift (¥30). Close to the park's main gate is the Azure Clouds Temple (Biyun Si), guarded by the menacing deities Heng and Ha in the Mountain Gate Hall. A series of farther halls leads to the Sun Yat Sen Memorial Hall, where the revolutionary leader's coffin was stored in 1925, before being taken to his final resting place in Nanjing. § Wofosi Lu • 6259 1155 • Bus: 331 from Summer Palace or 634 from Xizhi Men • Open 6am–6:30pm daily • ¥10, Azure Clouds Temple ¥10

Yuanming Yuan (Old Summer Palace)

4 Great Bell Temple (Dazhong Temple)

The 18th-century Da Zhong Si follows a typical Buddhist plan, with a Heavenly Kings Hall, Main Hall, and a Guanyin Bodhisattva Hall. What distinguishes it, though, is the 46.5 ton (47, 250 kg) bell – one of the world's largest – that is housed in the rear tower. The bell was cast between 1403 and 1424 and Buddhist *sutras* in Chinese and Sanskrit cover its surface. Hundreds more bells can be seen in another hall on the west side of the complex. ⊗ *31A Beisanhuan Xi Lu • Map B1 • 6255 0819 • Subway: Dazhangsi • Open 8:30am–9:30pm daily • ¥10*

5 Beijing Botanical Gardens

About a mile (2 km) northeast of Xiang Shan Park lie these pretty gardens, containing some 3,000 plant species and some pleasant walks. The garden's Sleeping Buddha Temple (Wofo Si) is renowned for its magnificent 15-ft (5-m) bronze statue of a reclining Buddha. China's last emperor, Pu Yi *(see p9)*, ended his days here as a gardener. ⊗ *6259 1283 • Bus: 331 from Summer Palace or 634 from Xizhi Men • Open 7am–5pm daily • ¥5 • www.beijingbg.com*

6 China Ethnic Culture Park

A theme park devoted to all of China's ethnic minorities *(see box)*, the complex is crammed

China Ethnic Culture Park

with a wonderful array of buildings such as the distinctive circular dwellings of the southern Hakka people, some of which are full-size replicas, while others are scale models. There is also a Chinese Song and Dance Theatre featuring daily performances by ethnic representatives in full costume. If you aren't traveling around the country, this is a fine way to get an idea of the diversity of China. ⊗ *1 Minzu Yuan Lu • Map E1 • 6206 3640 • Subway: Olympic Sports Center • Open 9am–7pm daily • ¥60 • www.emuseum.org.cn*

7 Science and Technology Museum

Exhibits begin with ancient science, highlighting China's "technological pre-eminence in history." The technology comes up to date with Chinese space capsules, robots, and an Astro-vision Theater incorporating state-of-the-art cinematography. The museum provides good educational fun for both young and old. ⊗ *1 Beisanhuan Zhong Lu • Map E1 • 6237 1177 • Subway: Beitucheng • Open 9am–4:30pm Tue–Sat • ¥30 • www.cstm.org.cn*

8 China National Film Museum

Reportedly the world's largest, this film museum is housed in a modern glass-and-steel structure adjacent to the Caochangdi Art District and features 20 exhibition halls, an IMAX theater, a digital

China's Peoples

China's 1.35 billion population includes about 55 different ethnic minorities, each with their own distinctive customs and, in many cases, languages. Though rich in culture, and varied, together they make up only seven percent of the population, with the main group, known as Han Chinese, accounting for the rest.

projection theater, and several 35mm theaters. Over one hundred years of Chinese cinema are represented by 1,500 films and 4,300 stills from the works of 450 film-makers. ◈ *9 Nanying Road, Caochangdi Village, Chaoyang • 8435 5959 • Bus: 418 from Dong Zhi Men • Open 9am–4:30pm Tue–Sun (last adm 3:30pm) • ¥20 • www.cnfm.org.cn*

798 Art District
Although it's called the 798 Art District (known locally as Da Shan Zi), Factory number 798 is only one of the several former industrial units taken over by artists and galleries. Although increasingly gentrified, the 798 still features many of Beijing's best galleries, including UCCA and Pace *(see pp24–5 & 49)*.

China Railway Museum
The last passenger steam services in China came to an end in 2006, but located northeast of the 798 Art District is this museum with a sizeable collection of old locomotives. Some of the cabs can be boarded, an exhibition on the history of China's railways is on display, and some of the machines will occasionally be in steam. Also, the engines are a must for boys of all ages. ◈ *1 Jiuxian Qiao Bei Lu • Map H1 • 6438 1317 • Open 9am–4pm Tue–Sun • ¥20, free for kids under 1.2 m*

China Railway Museum

Green Beijing

Morning

🕐 Be at the East Gate (Dong Men) of the **Summer Palace** for 8:30am to beat both the heat (if you are visiting in summer) and the crowds. Make your way along the north shore of Kunming Lake via the **Long Corridor** and ascend **Longevity Hill**. Descend again to the Marble Boat and take a pleasure cruiser across the lake to **South Lake Island**. Cross back to the mainland via the supremely elegant **Seventeen-arch Bridge**; from here it's a short walk north to exit where you came in at the East Gate. In the car park pick up a taxi and instruct the driver to take you to **Xiang Shan Gongyuan**, otherwise known as Fragrant Hills Park. Before you enter, **Sculpting In Time** is a café near the East Gate that does good salads, pastas, and pizza.

Afternoon

From the park's East Gate turn right for the **Temple of Brilliance**, built in 1780 and ransacked by Western troops in 1860 and 1900. Close by is the **Liuli Pagoda**, with bells hanging from its eaves that chime in the breeze. Continue north to pass between two small round lakes linked by a small hump-backed bridge – the whole known as the **Spectacles Lakes**. Beyond is a **chair lift** that takes you up to the top of the "Fragrant Hill". Zigzag back down past many more pavilions to arrive at the **Fragrant Hills Hotel**, designed by Chinese-American architect I.M. Pei, best known for his glass pyramid at the Louvre in Paris and the Suzhou Museum near Shanghai.

Left **Marco Polo Bridge** Right **Great Palace Gate, Ming Tombs**

Trips Out of Town

BEIJING HAS MORE THAN ENOUGH SIGHTS *to keep the average visitor busy, but after traveling all this way, it would be a shame not to grasp the opportunity to get out of the city. Of course, the Great Wall is an absolute must, but not far from the city are also ancient temples nestled on green hillsides and the vast necropolises of the Ming and Qing emperors. To the southwest is the 300-year-old stone Marco Polo Bridge and neighboring Wanping, a rare surviving example of a walled city. Both are an easy suburban bus ride from the city. Otherwise, most Beijing hotels organize tours to these sights.*

Spirit Way at the Ming Tombs

🔟 Sights

1. Great Wall
2. Ming Tombs
3. Eastern Qing Tombs
4. Western Qing Tombs
5. Cuandixia
6. Tanzhe Temple
7. Stupa Forest Temple
8. Marco Polo Bridge
9. Peking Man Site
10. Shidu

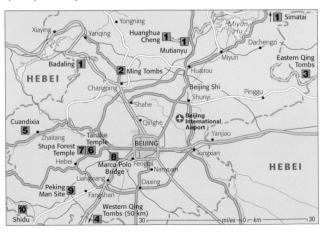

The Great Wall, snaking over high ridges north of Beijing

Great Wall
A visit to the wall is an absolute must. The closest section to Beijing is at Badaling, and you can get there and back in half a day. However, if you suspect that your appreciation of this matchless monument would be improved by the absence of coach-loads of fellow tourists, then considering traveling that little bit farther to the sites at Mutianyu, Huanghua Cheng, and Simatai (see pp28–9).

Ming Tombs
The Ming Tombs are the resting place for 13 of the 16 Ming emperors. These are Confucian shrines and follow a standard layout of a main gate leading to a series of courtyards and a main hall, with a "soul tower" and burial mound beyond. The tombs are not as colorful and elaborate as Buddhist and Daoist structures, and only three have been restored and are open to the public, however the necropolis is definitely a worthwhile stop-off as part of an excursion to the Great Wall (see pp26–7).

Eastern Qing Tombs
The remoteness of the Eastern Qing Tombs, over the border in Hebei province, makes them far less popular than their Ming counterparts, despite the fact that the setting is even more splendid. In fact, the Eastern Qing Tombs make up the largest and most complete imperial cemetery in China, built on a scale as grand as the Forbidden City. Of the many tombs here, only five are the burial places of Qing emperors, but there are also 14 empresses, and 136 imperial consorts. Notable are the tomb of the Qianlong Emperor, with an incredible tomb chamber adorned with Buddhist carvings, and the lavish tomb of the devious Empress Cixi (see p23). ◈ 77 miles (125 km) E of Beijing, Zuahua County, Hebei Province • Open May–Oct 8am–5pm daily; Nov–Apr 9am–4:30pm daily

Spirit Tower, Ming Tombs

 Most sights outside of Beijing have little to offer in the way of dining options, so it's wise to pack your own food

Trips Out of Town

Marco Polo

Whether Venetian trader and explorer Marco Polo (1254–1324) ever visited China is much disputed. The book he dictated to a ghost writer, who embroidered it substantially, describes aspects of Far Eastern life in much detail, including paper money, the Grand Canal, the structure of a Mongol army, tigers, and the bridge that now bears his name. *The Travels of Marco Polo*, however, may be based on earlier journeys by his father and uncles, and stories from Arab Silk Road merchants.

Western Qing Tombs

If few tourists ever visit the Eastern Qing Tombs, fewer still make it out here to their equally distant western counterparts. This vast burial complex comprises over 70 tombs in all, set in spectacular surroundings. Tombs include those of the emperors Daoguang, Guangxu, Jiaqing, and Yongzheng (r. 1723–35). It was the latter who founded this particular necropolis, perhaps because he could not bear to be buried beside his father, whose will he had thwarted when he seized the throne from his brother. In a nearby commercial cemetery are the remains of Pu Yi, the last emperor of China (see p9). ◈ *68 miles (110 km) SW of Beijing, Yixian County, Hebei Province • Open May–Oct 8am– 6pm daily; Nov–Apr 8am–5pm daily • ¥122 (Apr–Oct), ¥82 (Nov–Mar), Temple ¥15*

Cuandixia

On a steep mountainside, Cuandixia is a crumbling but picturesque hamlet of courtyard houses *(siheyuan)*, most dating from the Ming and Qing dynasties. An entry ticket allows access to the entire village, all of which can be explored in a few hours. The population consists of about 70 people spread over a handful of families. Accommodation with one of the families can be provided for those wanting an experience of rural hospitality. ◈ *Near Zhaitang town, 56 miles (90 km) W of Beijing • 6981 9333 • Subway to Pingguo Yuan (1 hr), then taxi, or bus 929 (2.5 hrs, twice daily) • ¥20*

Tanzhe Temple

This enormous temple dates back to the 3rd century AD, when it was known as Jiafu Si. It was later renamed for the adjacent mountain, Tanzhe Shan. It has a splendid mountainside setting, and its halls rise up the steep incline. The temple is especially famous for its ancient trees. There are no restaurants in the area, so bring your own lunch. ◈ *28 miles (45 km) W of Beijing • 6086 2505 • Subway to Pingguo Yuan (1 hr), then bus 931 or tourist bus 7 • Open 8am–5pm daily • ¥55*

Stupa Forest Temple

Near the parking lot for the Tanzhe Temple is this even more

Cuandixia village

fascinating temple, notable for its marvelous collection of brick stupas hidden among the foliage. Each stupa was constructed in memory of a renowned monk. The towering edifices were built in a variety of designs, and the earliest among them dates from the Jin dynasty (1115–1234).

⚲ *28 miles (45 km) W of Beijing • 6086 2505 • Subway to Pingguo Yuan (1 hr), then bus 931 or tourist bus 7 • Open 8am–5pm daily • ¥55*

Marco Polo Bridge

Straddling the Yongding River near Wanping town, the 876-ft (267-m) marble bridge was first built during the Jin dynasty in 1189 but was destroyed by a flood. The current structure dates to 1698. The bridge acquired its name when legendary voyager Marco Polo described it in his famous treatise *The Travels*. The balustrades along the length of the bridge are decorated by more than 400 stone lions, each one slightly different from all the others. On July 7, 1937, the Japanese Imperial Army and Nationalist Chinese soldiers exchanged fire at the bridge, an incident that led to the Japanese occupation of Beijing and war.

⚲ *10 miles (16 km) SW of Beijing • Bus 339 from Beijing's Lianhuachi bus station • Open 7am–7pm daily*

Peking Man Site (Zhoukoudian)

In the 1920s, archeologists removed from a cave at Zhoukoudian some 40-odd fossilized bones and primitive implements, which they identified as the prehistoric remains of Peking Man. It was thought that this exciting discovery provided the much sought-after link between Neanderthals and modern humans. Designated a

Stupa Forest Temple

UNESCO World Heritage site, the area is geared toward specialists, although the small museum has an interesting collection of tools and bone fragments. Peking Man himself is not here – his remains mysteriously disappeared during World War II. ⚲ *30 miles (48 km) SW of Beijing • 6930 1278 • Bus 917 from Beijing's Tianqiao station to Fangshan, then taxi • Open 8:30am–5pm daily • ¥35*

Shidu

Shidu offers a fabulous escape from the commotion of urban Beijing and a chance to enjoy some stunning natural scenery. Before the new road and bridges were built, travelers had to cross the Juma River ten times as they journeyed through the gorge between Shidu and nearby Zhangfang village, hence the name Shidu, which means "Ten Crossings." Pleasant walking trails wind along the riverbank between impressive gorges and limestone formations. ⚲ *62 miles (100 km) SW of Beijing • 6134 9009 • Train daily from Beijing's West Railway station to Shidu*

STREETSMART

BEIJING'S TOP 10

Above left to right **Spring, summer, fall, and winter in Beijing**

TOP 10 Planning Your Visit

1 When to Go
Spring and fall are the best times to visit. Summer is unbearably hot, while winter is fiercely cold. Planning your trip to coincide with one of the major festival periods *(see pp34–5)* can lead to a colorful trip, although tourist sights will be swamped.

2 Length of Stay
You need at least four full days to take in the highlights (the Forbidden City, Temple of Heaven, Summer Palace, and Great Wall). Six or seven days would allow you to experience the best of Beijing at a more comfortable pace.

3 What to Bring
November through March you need a coat, gloves, sweaters, thermal leggings, sturdy footwear, and lip balm. In summer, you need only loose-fitting shirts or T-shirts and thin trousers. Also bring a raincoat, sun hat, and reading material, as English-language books aren't easy to come by.

4 Visas and Passports
A passport, valid for at least six months, and a visa are needed to enter China. Its embassies and consulates issue a standard single-entry, 30-day visa, although longer-stay multiple-entry visas can also be obtained. Contact your nearest Chinese consulate or embassy for up-to-date information on visa restrictions.

5 Immunizations
Ensure that all of your routine vaccinations, such as tetanus, polio, and diphtheria, are up to date. It is also wise to get vaccinated against hepatitis A and B, typhoid, meningococcal meningitis, and cholera. Visitors traveling from yellow-fever hotspots must provide proof of vaccination against the disease.

6 Customs
Visitors to China are entitled to a duty-free allowance of two 75-cl bottles of wine or spirits and 400 cigarettes. Foreign currency exceeding US$5,000, or its equivalent, must be declared. It is not advisable to take in politically controversial literature, especially if it is written in Chinese. Special invoices or export licenses are required to take cultural relics out of China.

7 Language
The official language of China is Putonghua, known outside China as Mandarin. Putonghua is the native language of the north, but it is used across the country for communication between speakers of several other Chinese languages. English is not widely spoken outside of hotels.

8 Health Matters
Take out medical insurance before you travel. Beijing has private hospitals, but they are expensive. Pharmacies *(yaodian)*, identified by green crosses, are plentiful. They stock both Western and Chinese medicine, and can treat you for minor ailments. Avoid tap water – drink bottled water instead.

9 Security
Beijing is generally safe, and foreign visitors are unlikely to be the victims of crime, apart from petty theft and the occasional scam. Friendly Chinese who suggest a chat over tea may be in cahoots with a bar or café and looking to land you with a pumped-up bill. Hotels are reliably secure, but managements don't accept responsibility should anything vanish. Be discreet when taking out your wallet, and take care of your belongings at crowded tourist sites.

10 Local Prices
In general, prices are cheap. Admission to most sights (the Forbidden City and Great Wall excepted) is less than a dollar. If you avoid hotel restaurants, you can eat well for under $10 a head. Taxis are cheap enough to be a viable way of getting around; expect to pay the equivalent of two or three dollars for most short trips around town.

Above **Local newspapers and magazines**

Sources of Information

1 Tourist Information

China has yet to realize the value of professional tourist information centers. Those in Beijing are underfunded and poorly staffed.

2 Websites

There are many sites offering information on Beijing, and China in general. The best starting point is www.beijingpage. com, which is a gateway to many other useful sites. The official Beijing Tourism Administration site (www.bjta.gov.cn) is good for what's going on in the city. The websites of local event magazines, such as www.beijingtimeout.com, www.cityweekend.com. cn and www.thebeijinger. com, are better still.

3 Foreign Newspapers and Magazines

Foreign press is hard to come by, with just a small selection available in some of the larger hotels. You can usually get *Time*, *Newsweek*, the *International Herald Tribune*, and *Asian Wall Street Journal* – providing none of them carry articles critical of China.

4 Local Newspapers and Magazines

The government's English-language mouth-piece is *China Daily*. More worthwhile are the many English-language magazines aimed at expats and distributed free around the city's bars and restaurants. These include *The Beijinger*, *Time Out Beijing*, *Agenda*, and *City Weekend*; they are published fortnightly or monthly.

5 English-Language TV and Radio

The state-run Chinese Central Television (CCTV) has CCTV9 as its flagship English-language station. Cable and satellite television with BBC and CNN is available in top-end hotels. The Chinese radio network has only a few local English-language programs.

6 Guides and Maps

The tourist information offices offer only maps of the inner city. However, street vendors sell bigger ones for ¥1. Local English-language magazines often include useful maps too. Given the amount of changes taking place, it's vital that you buy the most recent map you can find. Anything more than just two or three years old will be of little use.

7 Business Information

The first place to start is the trade section of your own embassy in Beijing. Otherwise there are several trade promotion organizations including the American Chamber of Commerce, the British Chamber of Commerce, and the China Council for the Promotion of International Trade.

8 Background Reading: Photography

Edited by Pulitzer Prize-winning photographer Liu Heung Sing, *Portrait of a Country* traces the history of China through stunning photographs.

9 Background Reading: Non-fiction

Mr China by Tim Clissold is a terrific account of how to lose millions of dollars doing business with Beijing. *Mao* is Jung Chang's lacerating biography of the Great Leader, banned in China. *Foreign Babes in Beijing* by Rachel DeWoskin is the memoir of a sexually liberated American girl gatecrashing modern Chinese society. Paul French's *Midnight in Peking* is an atmospheric account of 1930s Beijing.

10 Background Reading: Fiction

Balzac and the Little Chinese Seamstress by Dai Sijie is a novella about the lives of two childhood friends enduring Mao's Cultural Revolution. *Wild Swans* by Jung Chang is a gripping story of three generations of women living through 20th-century China. Jiang Rong's *Wolf Totem* tracks the author's journey to Inner Mongolia, where he was sent during the Cultural Revolution.

Note: *The emergency hotline at Beijing's United Family Hospital is 5927 7120*

Left **By bicycle** Center **By taxi** Right **By bus**

TOP 10 Getting Around

1 Beijing Airport
On arrival visitors must complete an immigration form, submitted to officials at the customs desk. Here there are ATMs, foreign exchange counters, public telephones, left-luggage services, over-priced restaurants, and a limited number of shops.

2 From the Airport into Town
The Airport Express train costs only ¥25 and travels to Dongzhimen in 25 minutes, while a taxi ride to downtown Beijing may easily cost as much as ¥100–150.

3 Subway
The subway is a swift way to get around. Lines generally operate 6am–10:30pm. Tickets cost ¥2 per ride. If you plan to travel a lot, get a refillable blue magnetic card (¥20 deposit).
✪ www.explorebj.com

4 Buses
The city bus network is extensive and cheap. Most trips within the city center require a flat fare, which is clearly posted on the side of the bus; typically ¥1 or ¥2. A refillable blue card will reduce the cost down to 4 *jiao*. However, near-perpetual traffic jams mean bus journeys can often be lengthy. In addition, buses are almost always over-crowded and destinations are given in Chinese only. ✪ www.bjbus.com
• Hotline: 96166

5 Taxis
Taxis are abundant and can be hailed easily in the street. Official taxis are yellow, with stripes; avoid the illegal black ones. Make sure the driver uses the meter, which they usually only start once the journey is actually under way – so wait a moment, then say, "Dabiao" (meter), if necessary. Few taxi drivers speak English, so have your destination written down in Chinese by your hotel staff. Fares per kilometer (half mile) are posted on the side of the car. Prices start at ¥10 for the first three kilometers, then go up by ¥2 per kilometer. There is a surcharge after 11pm.

6 Cycling
Cycling can be a great way to explore. Bike lanes are common and roadside repair stalls are everywhere. Beijing is flat and very cyclable, but due to the heavy traffic, cycling here can be intimidating. Handy bike stands are found all over and have an attendant to watch the bikes for a modest fee.

7 Rickshaws
Bicycle rickshaws, once common in Beijing, are now relegated to the lakeside area of Hou Hai, north of the Forbidden City, where they offer tours of the old *hutongs* (alleys) to tourists.

8 Walking
Beijing is not a great city for walking. Most streets are inhumanely wide and traffic pollution can be choking. Exceptions include the Hou Hai area and the embassy districts of Ri Tan Park and Sanlitun. Parks such as Bei Hai, Chaoyang, Di Tan, and the Temple of Heaven Park, are also good places for strolling.

9 Tours
Most hotels in Beijing organize tours around the major city sights, as well as out of town to the Ming Tombs and Great Wall. Usually you don't have to be staying at the hotel in question to sign up for an excursion. If you want to tour the city independently, be aware that car rental agencies do not accept European driving licenses. However, you can hire a driver through local agencies such as BCC (www.bccrental.com).

10 Waterways
During the summer months, tour boats ply the city's ancient canal system. From 10am to 4pm there are sailings on the hour from Yuyuan Tan Park, near the Millennium Monument, and from the Beijing Exhibition Hall *(see p92)*, out to the Summer Palace.

Left **Automated tellers** Center **Sidewalk card telephones** Right **Chinese** *renminbi*

Banking and Communications

1 Currency
China's currency is called *yuan*, also written as *renminbi* and referred to in spoken language as *kuai*. One *yuan* divides into 10 *jiao* (or *mao*). The most common coins include 1 *yuan*, and 5 and 1 *jiao*. Bills in circulation are 1, 2, and 5 *jiao*, and 1, 2, 5, 10, 20, 50, and 100 *yuan*.

2 Changing Money
It is possible to exchange currency at major banks and international airports. Most decent hotels will change money, but for guests only. Exchange rates are decided centrally. Convert any left-over *renminbi* back before you leave, although usually only exchange counters at airports and ports will do this. You must present recent exchange or ATM receipts for double the amount you want to re-exchange. It is not advisable to change money at an unofficial agency.

3 Automated Tellers
There are many usable ATMs in banks, shopping malls, and hotels around the city center. Banks can be found all over town, and they generally accept Cirrus, Plus, American Express, Visa, and MasterCard cards. The limit per withdrawal is ¥2,000–¥2,500.

4 Credit Cards
Credit cards are widely accepted in upscale restaurants and top-end hotels, and in large tourist shops, but always check before attempting to make a purchase. The commonly accepted cards are MasterCard, Visa, JCB, Diners Club, and American Express.

5 Traveler's Checks
Some hotel foreign exchange counters no longer exchange checks, and will send you to the Bank of China. All popular foreign brands are accepted, but occasionally cashiers will reject those that look unfamiliar. Keep the proof of purchase slips and a record of the serial numbers in case of loss or theft.

6 Post
It may take as little as four days or as long as two months to send airmail and postcards overseas. Visitors can send mail by standard or registered post, while EMS (Express Mail Service) is a reliable way to send packages and documents, both abroad and within the country. However, contents will be inspected before sending. DHL and UPS have several branches in Beijing for express deliveries.

7 Telephones
International and long-distance phone calls can be made from most hotels and card telephones. It is usually necessary to ask receptionists or operators to place the calls. In cheaper hotels you may be asked to first pay a deposit. Most public phones require an IC (integrated circuit) card, sold in shops and kiosks wherever the letters "IC" are seen.

8 Calling Beijing
To call China from abroad, dial your international access code, China's country code 86, then 10 for Beijing, followed by the local number.

9 Mobiles
Visitors with mobile phones from almost anywhere except North America and Japan can use the Chinese system (Americans can only use the Chinese system if they have an unlocked tri- or quad-band phone). Just buy a local pre-paid SIM card from any phone shop. If you do not have a phone compatible with the Chinese system, the cheapest option is to buy one, not rent.

10 Internet Cafés
Upscale hotels and many cafés in Beijing (including all Starbucks) have Wi-Fi, and it is common to open one's laptop over a cup of cappuccino. Blocked sites can be accessed through a proxy server.

Left **Young Beijingers on Wangfujing** Right **Monk at the Lama Temple**

Etiquette

1 Greeting People
Shaking hands is commonplace and certainly considered the norm with foreign visitors. The usual Chinese greeting is "Ni hao," which means "How are you?" or "Nimen hao" in its plural form, to which you reply "Ni hao" or "Nimen hao."

2 Personal Questions
Although unfailingly polite, Chinese people will not blanch at asking you how much you earn, how old you are, or whether you are married. Such questions are seen as nothing more than taking a friendly interest in a new acquaintance.

3 Exchanging Business Cards
When proffering business cards, the Chinese do so using the fingertips of both hands, and receive cards in the same manner. For businessmen a good supply of cards is essential, preferably with English on one side and Chinese on the reverse.

4 Face
Although reserved in manner and expression, the Chinese also harbor strong feelings of personal pride and respect. The maintenance of pride and avoidance of shame is a concept known as "face." Loss of face creates great discomfort and major embarrassment for the Chinese, so although you may occasionally become frustrated by the incompetence of hotel staff, it is never a good idea to embarrass anybody in public.

5 Places of Worship
Buddhist, Daoist, and Confucian temples are relaxed about visitors wandering about, but you should be considerate toward worshipers and the resident monks, and refrain from sticking cameras in their faces. You need to dress more respectfully for mosques – avoid wearing shorts or short skirts, and cover your upper arms.

6 Staring
The Chinese habit of staring can be a little annoying. This sort of behavior is normally encountered in smaller towns and rural areas, but you also come across it in Beijing, since the city attracts a lot of migrant workers and peasant tourists. However, the intent is never hostile. Foreigners may also be asked to pose in photographs with the locals.

7 Tipping
The Chinese do not tip so neither should you, and that goes for guides, bell boys, taxi drivers, and anyone else. In China the price you agree for the service is the one you pay, although some restaurants in larger hotels now routinely add a service charge. Away from hotels and tourist areas waitresses will pursue you down the street to return the change they think you've forgotten.

8 Begging
China's imbalanced economic progress and huge population of rural poor have resulted in large numbers of beggars, especially in Beijing and other big cities. Foreign visitors are associated with wealth and naturally attract lots of attention, and groups of children are often sent by their parents to extract money. The best strategy is to ignore them and walk away.

9 Political Discussion
Avoid political discussion altogether. Most Chinese are uncomfortable hearing criticism of their leadership or nation. At the same time, they are quite happy to have a go at other countries, often to the point where you might feel provoked. Don't respond. Far better to just change the subject.

10 Chinese Names
The Chinese will usually state their last name first, followed by the given name. For example, Zhang Yimou, in Chinese would be Mr. Yimou Zhang using the Western style.

Above **Rush hour**

TOP 10 Things to Avoid

1 Students of English

So-called "language students" on the street will sometimes strike up conversation in order, so they will tell you, to practice their English. However, caution is necessary as increasingly these approaches are lead-ins to scams. These students may suggest entering a nearby teahouse, where you will naturally offer to buy them a drink. The students take generous advantage of your offer and then depart leaving you with a wildly inflated bill for thousands of *renminbi*. Of course, the bar owner is in on the deal.

2 Queuing

Despite the re-education measures taken up in the run-up to the Olympics, the Chinese don't do queues. They prefer to push and shove. People who politely wait their turn at the ticket office are likely to stand there all day.

3 Taking Offense at Spitting

Despite the best attempts of public educators, spitting remains a fact of Chinese life on the streets, buses and trains. It is not just an old man thing either; it is not uncommon to observe a pretty young woman break off mid-conversation to loudly expel a gob of saliva.

4 Rush Hour

Beijing's traffic is horrendous, and if you aren't careful you could spend half your visit sitting in a taxi, grid-locked in a sea of other vehicles. Rush hour seems to last nearly all day, but the roads are noticeably worse on week days before 10am and between around 5pm and 8pm. You should avoid traveling at these times if at all possible.

5 Art Students

Around Wangfujing Dajie, Liulichang, Tian'an Men Square and the Forbidden City, be wary of "art students" who in the guise of fund-raising will pressure you to visit an exhibition where you can buy amateur and hugely overpriced art.

6 Guides

At many of Beijing's sights, and particularly at the Forbidden Palace and Temple of Heaven, so-called guides wait around the ticket offices to offer their services. Decline. More often than not, they know little more than the bare facts, which are often recited with a dubious propagandist slant.

7 Visiting Sights on National Holidays

The biggest tourists in China are the Chinese themselves. On public holidays out-of-towners swarm into Beijing for a spot of sightseeing. It becomes impossible to move in the Forbidden City, Temple of Heaven, or in any of the parks.

8 Sweet and Sour Chicken

China's is one of the world's great cuisines. Chinese food is astonishing in its variety, and there is nowhere better to experience this than Beijing. The city boasts restaurants specializing in most, if not all, the country's many regional cuisines. Ordering the few Cantonese-originating dishes that have come to represent Chinese cooking to the rest of the world would really be a wasted opportunity.

9 Public Toilets

Even though some progress has been made, public toilets are hole-in-the-ground types, and they are usually extremely malodorous. You will also need to bring your own tissue paper. It is a better idea to take advantage of the facilities in top-end shopping malls, hotels, and restaurants.

10 Taking a Taxi without the Right Change

Beijing taxi drivers hardly ever seem to carry any change, so make sure you always have a good stash of ¥5, ¥10, and ¥20 notes to hand.

Always carry your passport, or a photocopy of your passport, and Chinese visa with you

Left **Exotic food at the Night Market** Right **Western-style restaurant**

Dining in Beijing

1 Restaurant areas
Beijing boasts literally thousands, if not tens of thousands, of restaurants. The best areas to wander in order to see what's on offer are around Hou Hai (see pp20–21) and along Ghost Street (see p87) for Chinese cuisine. For the widest choice of international restaurants, try the streets on the south side of Ri Tan Park (see p85) and those on the north and west sides of the Workers' Stadium (see p86) in the diplomatic and entertainment district of Sanlitun.

2 Strange foods
It is possible to find the likes of dog, snake, sea slug, scorpions, and penises from a variety of animals on the menus of Beijing restaurants. However, none of these are particularly common dishes, and you are unlikely to find them on the table in front of you without specifically seeking them out.

3 Chinese menus
Many restaurants have menus in Chinese only. In which case, it is perfectly acceptable to look around at what people on other tables are eating and just point to what you fancy.

4 International cuisine
Beijing is a modern, international city and many of its international restaurants are truly world class, notably those described on pages 60–61. If you should tire of Chinese cuisine, then without too much trouble you can find restaurants here that will do a great burger or an authentic spaghetti bolognese.

5 Eating with chopsticks
Chinese restaurants set their tables with chopsticks, not knives and forks. If you have never eaten with chopsticks before, try to get in a little practice before your visit to Beijing. Meals are placed in the middle of the table and shared by all. Food is eaten in the order in which the dishes are served.

6 Decor
Many Beijing restaurants appear very basic, even scruffy, with Formica tables, cheap furnishings, and plastic tableware. Chinese tend not to care about things like the aesthetics, the ambience, and the service. Instead what they care about is the quality of the food. Little else matters.

7 Street food
Chinese street food is plentiful, varied, and usually delicious (see p57). The best place to try it is at one of the two street-food markets off Wangfujing Dajie (see p71). There are also lots of street-food vendors in the Hou Hai area (see pp20–21).

8 Meal times
The Chinese tend to eat early. Lunch can be served as early as 11am and many restaurants will stop serving at 2pm. Dinner typically starts at around 5pm, with many restaurant kitchens closed by 9:30pm.

9 Late-night eating
Many of the hotel restaurants stay open late, as do a cluster of places around the west gate of the Workers' Stadium, notably the excellent Bellagio (see p58). A lot of bars serve decent food until the early hours, including The Tree (see p63), while most of the restaurants along Ghost Street (see p87) remain open 24 hours daily.

10 Dining with Chinese
As a guest of Chinese hosts it is polite to sample all of the dishes on the table, although you should leave something on the plate at the end of the meal. A clean plate indicates you are still hungry. Drinking is an important part of Chinese entertaining, but do not pour your own drink – it shows a lack of protocol. The most common expression for toasting is "Gan bei", meaning "dry the glass", or "bottoms up."

Left **Dazhalan street market** Right **Low-cost clothing at the Silk Market**

₀10 Shopping Tips

1 Opening hours
Most shops and markets are open from around 9am daily and do not close until around 9pm, or later.

2 Haggling
The Chinese haggle even in shops with fixed prices, and it pays for you to do the same. Haggling at markets is essential as traders will start by quoting you a price that can be 10 times or more beyond what is fair. Your first offer must always be a fraction of what they ask. For example, a trader who starts by demanding ¥150 for a jacket at the Silk Market will probably be prepared to let it go for as little as ¥20; offer ¥10 and then walk away, and listen as the price plummets.

3 Credit cards
Credit cards are becoming much more widely accepted in stores, restaurants, boutiques, and hotels and can also be used in ATMs at both Chinese and international banks. Always check just which cards are accepted and carry enough cash to cover you in case your plastic is rejected.

4 Fakes
Beijing is awash with fakes, from counterfeit Rolex watches to copies of North Face jackets. Some of these are extremely well done, with counterfeiters even going so far to replicate the internal workings of watches. Of course, it is illegal, and importing these goods may get you in trouble when re-entering your country.

5 Bargains
Counterfeit goods aside, there are few real bargains to be had in Beijing. No matter how good your haggling skills, no market trader ever sells at a loss, or even at anything like cost price. The antiques are anything but old, and even the Mao memorabilia is made specifically for the tourist trade. The simple rule is, buy something because you like it, not because you have been told that it is worth a great deal.

6 DVDs and CDs
With the price of a DVD (¥10–¥15) a fraction of the price of a cinema ticket, it is not surprising to see many more DVD stores than cinemas. Beijing is awash with pirate DVDs and CDs, sold openly from specialist stores. Movies appear on disc even before they've been premiered. Some of the less recent releases are highly professional, with all the added extras. However, some disks just won't play at all, or they might feature incomprehensible English subtitles. It's a bit of a gamble, and you can never be sure that the film you've just bought really contains what is advertised on the cover.

7 Tailoring
If you have the time and the inclination, one of the most satisfying shopping experiences is to buy some cloth and have a local tailor make up clothes to your own design or specifications. Present them with an example and they can make exact copies of your favorite shirts or trousers. They can even work from pictures in a magazine. Yashow (Yaxiu) Market *(see p88)* in Sanlitun has the greatest number of tailors, plus plenty of stalls selling cloth.

8 Refunds
Make sure that you really want what you're buying: there is no such thing as a refund in China.

9 Shopping areas
Beijing's main shopping thoroughfare is Wangfujing Dajie *(see p60)*. Other good places to shop include the Dazhalan and Liulichang *(see p73)* areas south of Tian'an Men Square, the Guomao area, Shin Kong Plaza, The Place, and Sanlitun.

10 Electronics
Don't mix up Beijing with Hong Kong: there are no bargain electronics here. Most hardware is imported and so costs significantly more than in your home country. You can get cheap Chinese-made equivalents, but these are unreliable and there is no warranty.

Left **Peninsula Palace Hotel** Right **Commune by the Great Wall**

🔟 Accommodation Tips

1 Area options
Distances in Beijing are vast, and roads are perpetually choked with traffic, so if you don't want to spend half your visit sitting in the back of a succession of taxis, be careful when choosing the location of your hotel. Unless business requires you to be elsewhere, then aim to stay as close to the Forbidden City as possible. In a choice of east side versus west, favor the former, since there are better restaurants and shopping opportunities.

2 Hotel standards
For international standards of comfort and service, stick to four- and five-star hotels managed by familiar Western chains, or opt for the Singapore- and Hong Kong-based luxury companies.

3 Star system
The Chinese star system of grading hotels is meaningless, since no star is ever lost once it has been given, despite sometimes dramatic deterioration.

4 Something different
Beijing now boasts a number of classy boutique and design hotels, and an even wider range of appealing courtyard hotels. The latter are conversions of traditional *siheyuan* (courtyard houses) in old *hutong* (alley) areas of the city. They vary in price and degree of comforts from budget to expensive luxury options. For a range of courtyard hotels in different price bands, *see p116*. Home stays options are also available.

5 Booking and bargaining
Online agencies such as www.ctrip.com or www.elong.net usually offer better rates than the ones found on a particular hotel's website. When contacting a hotel directly, always ask for a discount of the usually widely inflated rack rate quoted online. Most will be willing to reach a compromise on the price.

6 Payment
Even though credit cards have become increasingly widespread in Beijing, they are not universally accepted, so always ask whether they are a suitable form of payment when you check in. Hotel foreign exchange facilities are becoming less reliable, and holders of traveler's checks, in particular, may be sent to a bank. In more modest hotels, always be prepared to settle your bill in *renminbi*. Also, be aware that it is normal for most Chinese-run hotels to ask for payment of your room in advance.

7 Hidden extras
Service charges of between five and fifteen percent are frequently added to the final bill, so be sure to clarify this with reception staff at the start of your stay. Minibar contents are as overpriced in China as they are anywhere else; however, international telephone calls made from your room are subject to only a modest surcharge.

8 Seasonal demand
The busiest travel periods for the Chinese are during the three-day Labor Day holiday around May 1, the week-long National Day holiday around October 1, and the Chinese New Year *(see p34)*. If you are planning to be in China at any of these times, make any hotel (and domestic travel) reservations well in advance.

9 Traveling with kids
Most hotels allow children under the age of 12 to stay in their parents' room free of charge. Most will also add an extra bed for an older child for a nominal (and negotiable) fee.

10 Tipping
Traditionally, there is no tipping in China. Indeed, hotel staff may even try to return any money that is left for them.

If you are staying in a private home, you will need to register with the local police station within 24 hours of your arrival

Above: **Park Hyatt Beijing**

Price Categories		
For a standard, double room per night (with breakfast if included), taxes and extra charges.	¥	under ¥200
	¥¥	¥200–¥400
	¥¥¥	¥400–¥800
	¥¥¥¥	¥800–¥1400
	¥¥¥¥¥	over ¥1400

TOP 10 Luxury and Boutique Hotels

1 China World Summit Wing

Located in Beijing's tallest tower, this luxury hotel affords stunning 360° city views from its swish Atmosphere bar on the 80th floor. The four classy restaurants offer guests irresistible dining choices. There is also a spa and an infinity pool. ❧ *1 Jianguo Men Wai Dajie • Map H4 • 6505 2299 • Subway: Guomao • www.shangri-la. com/beijing • ¥¥¥¥¥*

2 Commune by the Great Wall

Outstanding villas by 12 renowned Asian architects dot a green valley within sight of the Great Wall. Facilities include DVD players, an indoor pool, and a superb Anantara Spa with terrace views over the valley. ❧ *Badaling, 30 miles (45 km) NW of Beijing • 8118 1888 • www. commune.com.cn • ¥¥¥¥¥*

3 Aman at the Summer Palace

Guests at this stunning hotel 6 miles (10 km) northwest of the city enjoy private access to the Summer Palace (*see pp22–3*) as well as a cinema, stylish spa, and subterranean swimming pool. ❧ *1 Gong Men Qian Jie • 5987 9999 • www. amanresorts.com • ¥¥¥¥¥*

4 Grace Beijing

Contemporary luxury best describes this stylish boutique hotel with 30 rooms, in the heart of the 798 Art District. Facilities include free Internet, a gym, bar, and the highly acclaimed Yi House French bistro – popular for its excellent weekend brunch. ❧ *Jiuxianqiao Lu, Zhao Yuan, 798 Art District • 6436 1818 • www. gracebeijing.com • ¥¥¥¥*

5 The Peninsula Beijing

Luxurious rooms have plasma TVs; marble bathrooms also have a small screen. Two terrific restaurants (Huang Ting and Jing), excellent service, a luxury mall, and a central location make this one of the city's best choices. ❧ *8 Jinyu Hutong • Map N4 • 8516 2888 • Subway: Dengshikou • www. peninsula.com • ¥¥¥¥¥*

6 Red Capital Residence

Beijing's quirkiest hotel has just five rooms, each furnished with period antiques and decorated according to a different theme. You can choose from the "Chairman's Suite" or one of the "Concubines' Private Courtyards". ❧ *66 Dong Si Liutiao • Map F2 • 8403 5308 • Subway: Dong Si Shi Tiao • www.redcapital club.com.cn • ¥¥¥¥¥*

7 The Opposite House

Designed by renowned Japanese architect Kengo Kuma, The Opposite House is part of The Village Sanlitun. Its 99 spacious rooms, all with natural wooden floors and deep oak soaking tubs, are a design experience, as is its stainless-steel pool. ❧ *11 Sanlitun Road • Map H2 • 6417 6688 • Subway: Tuanjiehu • www.the oppositehouse.com • ¥¥¥¥¥*

8 Park Hyatt Beijing

High-end service and style are the watchwords here. Chic, contemporary accommodation as well as stylish bars and restaurants draw the most discerning of clients. ❧ *2 Jianguo Men Dajie • Map H4 • 8567 1234 • Subway: Guomao • beijing. park.hyatt.com • ¥¥¥¥¥*

9 The Ritz-Carlton, Beijing

A perfect retreat for both business and leisure, this 305-room deluxe hotel offers fine dining, excellent facilities for meetings and events, and a high-end spa. ❧ *83A Jianguo Lu, China Central Place, Chaoyang District • www.ritzcarlton. com • ¥¥¥¥¥*

10 Raffles Hotel

Constructed in 1901, Raffles Hotel offers a winning mixture of heritage, luxury, and comfort. In an excellent location at the bottom of Wangfujing, it is just a short walk from Tian'an Men Square. ❧ *33 Dong Chang'an Jie • Map M5 • 6526 3388 • Subway: Wangfujing • www.raffles. com • ¥¥¥¥¥*

Unless otherwise stated, all hotels listed above accept credit cards, have en-suite bathrooms, and air-conditioning

Left **Park Plaza Hotel** Right **Aloft Beijing**

🏆10 Business and High-end Hotels

1 Hilton Beijing Wangfujing

Spacious, open-plan rooms, warm service, and a large pool are a huge draw. A central location within walking distance of Tian'an Men Square and the Forbidden City is another key feature.
🗝 8 Wangfujing Dong Dajie
• Map M4 • 5812 8888
• Subway: Wangfujing
• www.hilton.com • ¥¥¥¥

2 Crowne Plaza

Comfortable rooms with tasteful decoration give onto a nine-story atrium. Reasonable value, and within walking distance of Wangfujing and the Forbidden City.
🗝 48 Wangfujing Dajie
• Map N3 • 5911 9999
• Subway: Wangfujing
• www.beijinghotels. crowneplaza.com • ¥¥¥¥

3 Park Plaza Hotel

The stylish Park Plaza is a peaceful oasis in a fast developing precinct. Rooms feature designer touches and the hotel is convenient for Wangfujing Dajie and the Forbidden City. 🗝 97 Jinbao Jie
• Map N3 • 8522 1999
• Subway: Wangfujing
• www.parkplaza.com/ beijingcn • ¥¥¥¥

4 Hotel G

Just five minutes' walk from the bright lights of Sanlitun, this boutique hotel is a stylish and well-priced bolthole. At night the hotel's facade is lit up with an array of

colored lights. Rooms are sleek and inviting.
🗝 A7 Gongti Xi Lu • Map G3 • 6552 3606 • www. hotel-g.com • ¥¥¥¥

5 Langham Place

Located near Beijing Capital Airport, this hotel offers luxury rooms and suites, several modern restaurants and bars, a club lounge, gym, free Wi-Fi, an art gallery, and free airport shuttle bus service. 🗝 1 Er Jing Rd, opp Terminal 3 • 6457 5555 • Subway: Beijing International Airport • www. beijingairport.langhamplace hotels.com • ¥¥¥¥

6 Kerry Center Hotel

The Kerry Center combines the Shangri-La group's high service standards with bright, modern room design. The Kerry is also home to the Centro cocktail bar (see p62) and extensive health facilities. 🗝 1 Guanghua Lu • Map H4 • 6561 8833
• Subway: Guomao • www. shangri-la.com • ¥¥¥¥¥

7 Hotel Kapok

Designed by famous Chinese architect Zhu Pei, in 2006 the Kapok was hailed as Beijing's first boutique hotel. It is close to both shopping areas and the Forbidden City, and has 89 rooms on five floors, all with spacious bathrooms; some have private gardens.
🗝 16 Donghua Men Dajie
• Map M4 • 6525 9988
• Subway: Dengshikou,

Tian'an Men Dong or Wangfujing • www.kapok hotelbeijing.com • ¥¥¥¥¥

8 East

Set in parkland in the INDIGO business district, this contemporary hotel caters to high-end business travelers. All 369 rooms and 23 executive suites have an iPod touch, LCD TV, free Wi-Fi, and iHome audio system. The hotel also has two restaurants, a pool, and gym facilities.
🗝 22 Jiuxianqiao Rd, Chaoyang • 6417 6688
• www.east-beijing.com
• ¥¥¥¥

9 The Westin Beijing Chaoyang

Outstanding service is complemented by stylish decor. Being set on a ring road is not ideal, but the main sights and shopping areas are a short taxi ride away. 🗝 7 Dong San Huan
• Map H1 • 5922 8888
• Subway: Liangma Qiao
• www.starwoodhotels. com • ¥¥¥¥¥

10 Aloft Beijing

Nestled in the heart of the university district, close to the Summer Palace and the Olympic Stadium, this funky, good-value hotel is aimed at young travelers. It offers free Wi-Fi, a lounge with a pool table, and a restaurant that is open 24 hours a day 🗝 Tower 2, 25 Yuanda Lu, Haidian
• 8889 8000 • www.aloft hotels.com/beijing • ¥¥¥¥

Unless otherwise stated, all hotels listed above accept credit cards, have en-suite bathrooms, and air-conditioning

Price Categories
For a standard, double room per night (with breakfast if included), taxes and extra charges.

¥	under ¥200
¥¥	¥200–¥400
¥¥¥	¥400–¥800
¥¥¥¥	¥800–¥1400
¥¥¥¥¥	over ¥1400

Above **Scitech Hotel**

🔟 Mid-range Hotels

Penta Beijing
Located close to Tian'an Men Square and the Temple of Heaven, this stylish hotel is suited for both business and leisure. As well as good business and modern in-room facilities with an accent on fun and informality, it offers a lounge, gym, games area and free Wi-Fi. ◈ *3–18 Chongwen Men Wai Dajie, Dongcheng • Map F5 • 6708 1188 • www. pentahotels.com • ¥¥¥*

Hade Men Hotel
Among the older hotels in Beijing, but renovated to a standard above other Chinese-run options in this range. Rooms are comfortable, if a bit gaudy, with nice views from the upper floors. It's round the corner from the railway station. ◈ *2A Chongwen Men Wai Dajie • Map N6 • 6711 2244 • Subway: Chongwen Men • ¥¥¥*

Red Hotel
Staying true to its name, the former Red House Hotel, stands out with its vibrant facade. This establishment offers clean, cheerful rooms, which are good value for money. There's a popular football bar on premises, and it's a short walk to more bars in the Sanlitun district. ◈ *10 Taiping Zhuang Chunxiu Lu • Map G2 • 6417 1066 • Subway: Dong Zhi Men • www. red-hotel.com • ¥¥*

Crystal Orange
This good-value hotel is furnished in bold colors with modern paintings and Marilyn Monroe portraits adorning the walls. Rooms are comfortable, have spacious bathrooms and feature all modern conveniences including Wi-Fi and iPod docks. ◈ *25 Yonganli Zhong Jie, Chaoyang • Map C4 • 6566 1515 • ¥¥¥*

City Hotel Beijing
Sound mid-range option within walking distance of Sanlitun's bars, restaurants, and shops. Rooms are clean and comfortable, if a little dated. Staff speak some English. ◈ *4 Gongren Tiyuchang Dong Lu • Map H2 • 6500 7799 • Subway: Dong Si Shi Tiao • www. cityhotel.cn • ¥¥¥¥*

Holiday Inn Express Dongzhimen
Centrally located between Dongzhimen and Gongti Bei Lu, this hotel offers rooms at affordable prices, with easy access to the city's main attractions. Breakfast is included in the room rate, as is Wi-Fi. ◈ *1 Chunxiu Lu, Dongcheng • Map G2 • 6416 9999 • Subway: Dong Zhi Men • www.hiexpress.com • ¥¥¥*

Motel 268
Because of its prime location, this branch of China's economy hotel chain Motel 168 has been branded Motel 268. The 156-room property offers four categories of rooms, all with Internet access, air conditioning, and TV. Make sure your room has a window. ◈ *19 Jin Yu Hutong • Map N4 • 5167 1666 • Subway: Deng Shi Kou • ¥¥-¥¥¥*

Huafeng Hotel
The Huafeng may be bland, but it offers good value for money in the pleasant Legation Quarter, and is walking distance from central Tian'an Men Square and Wangfujing Street. ◈ *5 Qian Men Dong Dajie • Map M6 • 6524 7311 • Subway: Qian Men • ¥¥¥-¥¥¥¥*

Scitech Hotel
A good-value option for both shoppers and hedonists, the four-star Scitech abuts a large department store and popular nightclub Banana. Standard rooms are a bit on the small side but are otherwise comfortable. ◈ *22 Jianguo Men Wai Dajie • Map G4 • 6512 3388 • Subway: Jianguo Men • www.scitechhotel. com • ¥¥¥*

Qian Men Jianguo Hotel
The hotel itself isn't much to look at, but rooms are decent. The Li Yuan Theater, with nightly shows of Beijing Opera, is on the hotel grounds. The Temple of Heaven is a short walk away. ◈ *175 Yong'an Lu • Map D6 • 6301 6688 • Subway: Heping Men • ¥¥¥-¥¥¥¥*

In Beijing's mid-range hotels credit cards are often not accepted and air-conditioning is not always standard. Check when booking

Left **Bamboo Garden Hotel** Right **Lu Song Yuan Hotel**

🔟 Courtyard Hotels

1 Duge Courtyard Hotel

Duge's 10 individually decorated suites are designed in a dramatic and decadent fashion, and hidden behind two imposing doors. The Peony Pavilion room is prettily classic, while other rooms are more contemporary. All are centred on one of several small courtyards. ◈ 26 Qianyuanensi Hutong, Nan Luogu Xiang • Map E2 • 6406 0686 • Subway: Anding Men • www.duge courtyard.com • ¥¥¥¥¥

2 Sweet Garden Hostel

Peaceful, family-run hostel in a converted courtyard residence close to Dong Si Shi Tiao subway offers simple single, double, and 4–6 bed dorm rooms. Staff speak little English but arrange bike hire, ticket booking services, and even airport pick-up. ◈ 19 Dong Si Qi Tiao • Map G2 • 6405 1538 • Subway: Dong Si Shi Tiao • ¥

3 4 Banqiao

Tucked away in Banqiao Hutong, this traditional courtyard-style guesthouse is located near Dongzhimen and Guijie (Ghost Street). It offers 18 clean rooms with traditional Chinese furniture. ◈ 4 Banqiao Hutong, Beixinqiao • Map F2 • 8403 0968 • Subway: Beixinqiao • www.4banqiao. com • ¥¥¥–¥¥¥¥

4 Bamboo Garden Hotel

Close to the lakes, this is the oldest of Beijing's traditional hotels, with the largest and most elaborate courtyards, plus rockeries and covered pathways. ◈ 24 Xiao Shi Qiao Hutong • Map E1 • 5852 0088 • Subway: Gulou Dajie • www.bbgh.com.cn • ¥¥¥

5 The Orchid

Located in the heart of old Beijing, this stylish *hutong* hotel offers 10 comfortable rooms with en-suite bathroom, TV and free Wi-Fi. The rooftop cocktail bar overlooks the Drum and Bell Towers. ◈ 65 Baochao Hutong, Dongcheng District • Map E1 • 8404 4818 • Subway: Gulou Dajie • www. theorchidbeijing.com • ¥¥¥

6 Courtyard 7

This small, tastefully decorated courtyard hotel is over 300 years old. Set back from an interesting *hutong*, it makes for a peaceful refuge. Rooms and bathrooms have been sympathetically modernized. ◈ 7 Qiangulouyuan Hutong, Nan Luogu Xiang • Map E2 • 6406 0777 • Subway: Anding Men • www.courtyard7.com • ¥¥¥

7 Lu Song Yuan Hotel

The details are similar to those in other courtyard hotels, but here they add up to a more comfortable atmosphere. Rooms range from cheap youth hostel-style facilities to suites. There's also a teahouse. ◈ 22 Banchang Hutong, Kuan Jie • Map N1 • 6404 0436 • Subway: Anding Men • www.the-silk-road. com • ¥¥¥

8 3 + 1 Bedrooms

It may be in one of the most historic parts of Beijing, but this tiny courtyard hotel goes all out to be modern, with chic, minimalist style and features like iPod docks and free Wi-Fi. ◈ 17 Zhangwang Hutong, Jiu Gulou Dajie • Map E1 • 6404 7030 • Subway: Gulou Dajie • www.3plus1 bedrooms.com • ¥¥¥¥

9 Kelly's Courtyard

This stylish hostel in a historic *hutong* near Xidan and the financial district is owned by a travel-loving Chinese fashion designer. ◈ 25 Xiaoyuan Hutong, off Bingmasi Hutong, Xidan North Street • Map C3 • 6611 8515 • Bus: 47, 105, 690, or 808 • www. kellyscourtyard.com • ¥¥¥

10 Red Lantern House

The Red Lantern House occupies a main building and two pretty court-yards. It is family-owned and only a stone's throw away from the bars of Hou Hai. ◈ 5 Zheng Jue Hutong, Xinjiekou Nan Dajie, Xicheng • Map D2 • 8328 5771 • Subway: Jishuitan • www.redlantern house.com • ¥–¥¥

In courtyard hotels credit cards are often not accepted and air-conditioning is not always standard. Check when booking

Price Categories
For a standard, double room per night (with breakfast if included), taxes and extra charges.

¥	under ¥200
¥¥	¥200–¥400
¥¥¥	¥400–¥800
¥¥¥¥	¥800–¥1400
¥¥¥¥¥	over ¥1400

Above **Templeside House Hostel**

🔟 Budget Hotels

1 Beijing City Youth Hostel

Good value and very convenient for those with early morning trains from Beijing Zhan. Twin rooms and dorms are neat and clean, and there are cooking facilities and a 24-hour shop. ◈ *1 Beijing Zhan Xijie • Map F4 • 6525 8066 • Subway: Beijing Railway Station • www.centralhostel.com • ¥*

2 Leo Hostel

Excellent location south of Tian'an Men Square, in among old lanes. Rooms range from 12-bed dorms to doubles; facilities range from bicycle hire to a second-hand book exchange. ◈ *Guang Ju Yuan, 52 Dazhalan Xijie • Map L6 • 6303 1595 • Subway: Qian Men • www.leohostel.com • ¥*

3 Downtown Backpackers

Good value in the heart of one of Beijing's most vibrant *hutongs*. It's also minutes from the lakes and myriad restaurants and bars. Offers clean single rooms, doubles with attached bath, and 6–8 bed dorms. ◈ *85 Nan Luo Gu Xiang • Map E2 • 8400 2429 • Subway: Anding Men • www. backpackingchina.com • ¥*

4 Far East International Youth Hostel

The city's most charming YHA hostel, with dorms and private rooms in hotel and courtyard settings. The area was an imperial-era red-light district and remains lively. ◈ *90 Tieshu Xie Jie • Map K6 • 5195 8811 • Subway: Heping Men • www.fareastyh.com • ¥*

5 Feiying International Youth Hostel

Among the cheapest of Beijing's HI hostels. Private twins and dorms are pristine, and staff are helpful. Facilities include a comfortable bar and restaurant. ◈ *10 Xuanwu Men Xi Dajie • Map C4 • 6317 1116 • Subway: Changchun Jie • ¥*

6 Saga International Youth Hostel

Featuring spotless doubles, triples, and dorm rooms, a communal kitchen and café, and a rooftop patio. Helpful English-speaking staff organize ticket bookings and tours. ◈ *9 Shijia Hutong • Map N3 • 6527 2773 • Subway: Deng Shi Kou • www.sagayouth hostelbeijing.cn • ¥*

7 Templeside House Hostel

This courtyard hostel gives budget travelers a glimpse of traditional Beijing life. It has single, double, and bunk bedrooms, as well as a courtyard garden. ◈ *8 An Ping Xiang, Zhao Deng Yu Lu • Map C3 • 6615 7797 • Subway: Fucheng Men • www.templeside.com • ¥*

8 Alley Garden Courtyard Hostel

Tucked away in a *hutong*, near the Lama Temple and Ghost Street, this hostel is a traditional courtyard home with nine Chinese-style rooms. ◈ *46 Beixinqiao Santiao, Dongcheng • Map F2 • 8401 5027 • Subway: Yonghe Gong • www. alleygardenhotel.com/ gyyhyj.asp • ¥¥*

9 Friendship Youth Hostel

In the middle of the Sanlitun bar district, this is the hostel if you like your accommodations loud and lively. Rooms are simple and share bathrooms, but facilities are clean. Breakfast and laundry are free and there's a raucous bar attached. To find the hostel, walk up the east side of Yashow (Yaxiu) Market and just keep going. ◈ *43 Sanlitun Bei Lu • Map H2 • 6417 2597 • Subway: Tuanjiehu • ¥¥*

10 Zhaolong International Youth Hostel

A quiet option despite the proximity to Sanlitun bar district and shopping area. Dorms are tidy, and guests have access to a self-catering dining room, games room, and bike rentals. The front door is locked at 1am nightly. ◈ *2 Gongti Bei Lu • Map H2 • 6597 2666 • Subway: Tuanjiehu • ¥¥*

Phrase Book

The Chinese language belongs to the Sino-Tibetan family of languages and uses characters which are ideographic – a symbol is used to represent an idea or an object. Mandarin Chinese, known as Putonghua in mainland China, is fairly straightforward as each character is monosyllabic. Traditionally, Chinese is written in vertical columns from top right to bottom left, however the Western style is widely used. There are several romanization systems; the Pinyin system used here is the official system in mainland China. This phrase book gives the English word or phrase, followed by the Chinese script, then the Pinyin for pronunciation.

Guidelines for Pronunciation

Pronounce vowels as in these English words:

a	as in "father"	
e	as in "lurch"	
i	as in "see"	
o	as in "solid"	
u	as in "pooh"	
ü	as the French u or German ü (place your lips to say oo and try to say ee)	

Most of the consonants are pronounced as in English. As a rough guide, pronounce the following consonants as in these English words:

c	as ts in "hats"
q	as ch in "cheat"
x	as sh in "sheet"
z	as ds in "heads"
zh	as j in "Joe"

Mandarin Chinese is a tonal language with four tones, represented in Pinyin by one of the following marks ‾ ´ ˇ ` above each vowel – the symbol shows whether the tone is flat, rising, falling and rising, or falling. The Chinese characters do not convey this information: tones are learnt when the character is learnt. Teaching tones is beyond the scope of this small phrase book, but a language course book with a cassette or CD will help those who wish to take the language further.

Dialects

There are many Chinese dialects in use. It is hard to guess exactly how many, but they can be roughly classified into one of seven large groups (Mandarin, Cantonese, Hakka, Hui etc.), each group containing a large number of more minor dialects. Although all these dialects are quite different – Cantonese uses six tones instead of four – Mandarin or Putonghua, which is mainly based on the Beijing dialect, is the official language. Despite these differences all Chinese people are more or less able to use the same formal written language so they can understand each other's writing, if not each other's speech.

In an Emergency

Help!	请帮忙！	Qing bangmang
Stop!	停住！	Ting zhu
Call a doctor!	叫医生！	Jiao yisheng
Call an ambulance!	叫救护车！	Jiao jiuhuche
Call the police!	叫警察！	Jiao jiingcha
Fire!	火！	Huo
Where is the hospital/police station?	医院/警察局在哪里？	Yiyuan/jingcha fenju zai nali?

Communication Essentials

Hello	你好	Nihao
Goodbye	再见	Zaijian
Yes/no	是 / 不是	shi/bushi
… not …	不是	bushi
I'm from…	我是… 人	Wo shi … ren
I understand	我明白	Wo mingbai
I don't know	我不知道	Wo bu zhidao
Thank you	谢谢你	Xiexie ni
Thank you very much	多谢	Duo xie
Thanks (casual)	谢谢	Xiexie
You're welcome	不用谢	Bu yong xie
No, thank you	不，谢谢你	Bu, xiexie ni
Please (offering)	请	Qing
Please (asking)	请问	Qing wen
I don't understand	我不明白	Wo Bu mingbai
Sorry/Excuse me!	抱歉／对不起	Baoqian/ duibuqi
Could you help me please? (not emergency)	你能帮助我吗？	Ni neng bang zhu wo ma?

Useful Phrases

My name is ….	我叫…	Wo jiao …
Goodbye	再见	Zaijian
What is (this)?	（这）是什么?	(zhe) shi shenme?
Could I possibly have …? (very polite)	能不能请你给我 …?	Neng buneng qing ni gei wo …
Is there … here?	这儿有 … 吗?	Zhe'r you … ma?
Where can I get …?	我在哪里可以得到 …?	Wo zai na li keyi de dao …?
How much is it?	它要多少钱?	Ta yao duoshao qian?
What time is …?	… 什么时间?	… shenme shijian
Cheers! (toast)	干杯	Ganbei
Where is the restroom/toilet?	卫生间 / 洗手间在哪里?	Weishengjian/ Xishoujian zai nali?

Signs

open	开	kai
closed	关	guan
entrance	入口	renkou
exit	出口	chukou
danger	危险	weixian
emergency exit	安全门	anquanmen
information	信息	xinxi
restroom/toilet (men)	卫生间 / 洗手间	Weishengjian/ Xishoujian
(women)	（男士）（女士）	(nanshi) (nüshi)
men	男士	nanshi
women	女士	nüshi

Money

bank	银行	yinhang
cash	现金	xianjin
credit card	信用卡	xinyongka
currency exchange office	外汇兑换处	waihui duihuanchu
dollars	美元	meiyuan
pounds	英镑	yingbang
yuan	元	yuan

Keeping in Touch

Where is a telephone?	电话在哪里?	Dianhua zai nali?
May I use your phone?	我可以用你的电话吗?	Wo keyi yong nide dianhua ma?
mobile phone	手机	shouji
sim card	sim 卡	sim ka
Hello, this is ...	你好，我是 ...	Nihao, wo shi
airmail	航空	hangkong
e-mail	电子邮件	dianzi youjian
fax	传真	chuanzhen
internet	互联网	hulianwang
postcard	明信片	mingxinpian
post office	邮局	youju
stamp	邮票	youpiao
telephone card	电话卡	dianhua ka

Shopping

Where can I buy ...?	我可以在哪里买到 ...?	Wo keyi zai nali maidao ...?
How much does this cost?	这要多少钱?	Zhe yao duoshao qian?
Too expensive!	太贵了!	Tai gui le!
Do you have ...?	你有 ... 吗?	Ni you ...?
May I try this on?	我可以试穿吗?	Wo keyi shi chuan ma?
Please show me that.	请给我看看那个。	Qing gei wo kankan na ge.

Sightseeing

Where is ...?	... 在哪里?	... zai nali?
How do I get to ...?	我怎么到 ...?	Wo zenme dao ...?
Is it far?	远不远?	Yuan bu yuan?
bridge	桥	qiao
city	城市	chengshi
city center	市中心	shi zhongxin
gardens	花园	huayuan
mountain	山	shan
museum	博物馆	bowuguan
palace	宫殿	gongdian
park	公园	gongyuan
port	港口	gangkou
river	江，河	jiang, he
ruins	废墟	feixu
shopping area	购物区	gouwu qu
shrine	神殿	shendian
street	街	jie
temple	寺 / 庙	si/miao
town	镇	zhen
village	村	cun
zoo	动物园	dongwuyuan
north	北	bei
south	南	nan
east	东	dong
west	西	xi
left/right	左 / 右	zuo/you
straight ahead	一直向前	yizhi xiangqian

Getting Around

airport	机场	jichang
bicycle	自行车	zixingche
I want to rent a bicycle	我想租一辆自行车。	Wo xiang zu yiliang zixingche.
ordinary bus	公共汽车	gonggong qiche
express bus	特快公共汽车	tekuai gonggong qiche
minibus	面包车	mianbaoche
main bus station	公共汽车总站	gonggong qiche zong zhan
Which bus goes to ...?	哪一路公共汽车到 ... 去?	Nayilu gonggong qiche dao ... qu?
Please tell me where to get off?	请告诉我在哪里下车?	Qing gaosu wo zai nali xia che.
car	小汽车	xiaoqiche
ferry	渡船	duchuan
baggage room	行李室	xingli shi
one-way ticket	单程票	dancheng piao
return ticket	往返票	wangfan piao
taxi	出租车	chuzuche
ticket	票	piao
ticket office	售票处	shoupiao chu
timetable	时刻表	shikebiao

Accommodations

air-conditioning	空调	kongtiao
bath	洗澡	xizao
check-out	退房	tui fang
deposit	定金	dingjin
double bed	双人床	shuangren chuang
hair drier	吹风机	chuifeng ji
room	房间	fangjian
economy room	经济房	jingji fang
key	钥匙	yaoshi
front desk	前台	qiantai
single/twin room	单人 / 双人房	danren/ shuangren fang
single beds	单人床	danren chuang
shower	淋浴	linyu
standard room	标准房间	biaozhun fangjian
deluxe suite	豪华套房	haohua taofang

Eating Out

May I see the menu?	请给我看看菜单。	Qing gei wo kankan caidan
Is there a set menu?	有没有套餐?	You meiyou taocan?
I'd like ...	我想要 ...	Wo xiang yao
May I have one of those?	请给我这个。	Qing gei wo zhege
I am a vegetarian	我是素食者。	Wo shi sushizhe

Waiter/waitress!	服务员！	Fuwuyuan!
May I have a fork/knife/spoon	请给我一把叉/刀/汤匙。	Qing gei wo yiba cha/dao/tangshi
May we have the check please.	请把帐单开给我们。	Qing ba zhangdan kaigei women
breakfast	早餐	zaocan
buffet	自助餐	zizhucan
chopsticks	筷子	kuaizi
dinner	晚餐	wancan
to drink	喝	he
to eat	吃	chi
food	食品	shipin
full (stomach)	饱	bao
hot/cold	热/冷	re/leng
hungry	饿	e
lunch	午餐	wucan
set menu	套餐	taocan
spicy	酸辣	suan la
hot (spicy)	辣	la
sweet	甜	tian
mild	淡	dan
Western food	西餐	xi can
restaurant	餐馆	canguan
restaurant (upscale)	饭店	fandian

Food

apple	苹果	pingguo
bacon	咸肉	xianrou
bamboo shoots	笋	sun
beancurd	豆腐	doufu
bean sprouts	豆芽	dou ya
beans	豆	dou
beef	牛肉	niurou
beer	啤酒	pijiu
bread	面包	mianbao
butter	黄油	huangyou
chicken	鸡	ji
crab	蟹	xie
duck	鸭	ya
eel	鳗	man
egg	蛋	dan
eggplant	茄子	qiezi
fermented soybean paste	酱	jiang
fish	鱼	yu
fried egg	炒蛋	chao dan
fried tofu	油豆腐	you doufu
fruit	水果	shuiguo
fruit juice	果汁	guo zhi
ginger	姜	jiang
ice cream	冰淇淋	bingqilin
meat	肉	rou
melon	瓜	gua
noodles	面	mian
egg noodles	鸡蛋面	jidan mian
wheat flour noodles	面粉面	mianfen mian
rice flour noodles	米粉面	mifen mian
omelet	煎蛋饼	jiandanbing
onion	洋葱	yangcong
peach	桃子	taozi
pepper	胡椒粉，辣椒	hujiaofen, lajiao
pickles	泡菜	paocai

pork	猪肉	zhurou
potato	土豆	tudou
rice	米饭	mifan
rice crackers	爆米花饼干	baomihua bing'gan
rice wine	米酒	mi jiu
salad	色拉	sala
salmon	鲑鱼，大马哈鱼	guiyu, damahayu
salt	盐	yan
scallion	韭葱	jiucong
seaweed	海带	haidai
shrimp	虾	xia
soup	汤	tang
soy sauce	酱油	jiangyou
squid	鱿鱼	youyu
steak	牛排	niupai
sugar	糖	tang
vegetables	蔬菜	shucai
yoghurt	酸奶	suannai

Drinks

beer	啤酒	pijiu
black tea	红茶	hong cha
coffee (hot)	（热）咖啡	(re) kafei
green tea	绿茶	lü cha
iced coffee	冰咖啡	bing kafei
milk	牛奶	niunai
mineral water	矿泉水	kuang quanshui
orange juice	橙汁	cheng zhi
wine	葡萄酒	putaojiu

Numbers

0	零	ling
1	一	yi
2	二	er
3	三	san
4	四	si
5	五	wu
6	六	liu
7	七	qi
8	八	ba
9	九	jiu
10	十	shi
11	十一	shiyi
12	十二	shier
20	二十	ershi
21	二十一	ershi yi
22	二十二	ershi er
30	三十	sanshi
40	四十	sishi
100	一百	yi bai
101	一百零一	yi bai ling yi
200	二百	er bai

Time

Monday	星期一	xingqiyi
Tuesday	星期二	xingqi'er
Wednesday	星期三	xingqisan
Thursday	星期四	xingqisi
Friday	星期五	xingqiwu
Saturday	星期六	xingqiliu
Sunday	星期天	xingqitian
today	今天	jintian
yesterday	昨天	zuotian
tomorrow	明天	mingtian

General Index

Acknowledgments

The Author
Andrew Humphreys is a travel writer and editor who recently spent six months exploring Beijing.

Produced BY BRAZIL STREET
Editorial Nancy Pellegrini, Andrew Humphreys
Design Gadi Farfour
Main Photographer Chen Chao
Photography Co-ordinator and Factchecking Amanda Mengpo Li
Proofreader Ferdie McDonald

AT DORLING KINDERSLEY
Series Publisher Douglas Amrine
Publisher Managers Vivien Antwi, Jane Ewart
Senior Editor Hugh Thompson
Cartography Co-ordinator Casper Morris
Picture Research Rachel Barber, Rhiannon Furbear, Ellen Root
DTP Designer Natasha Lu
Production Linda Dare
Revisions Team
Shruti Bahl, Marta Bescos Sanchez, Gary Bowerman, Emer Fitzgerald, Anna Freiberger, Camilla Gersh, Katharina Hahn, Helena Iveson, Stuart James, Claudia Kotte, Maite Lantaron, Hayley Maher, Helen Partington, Khushboo Priya, Rada Radojicic, Marisa Renzullo, Sands Publishing Solutions, Josh Summers, Ajay Verma.

Maps (DK India)
Senior Cartographer Suresh Kumar
Cartographer Mohammad Hassan

Additional Photography
Demetrio Carrasco, Eddie Gerald, Ian O'Leary, Colin Sinclair, Linda Whitwam

Picture Credits
Dorling Kindersley would like to thank all the many establishments covered in this book for their assistance and kind permission for the producers to take photographs.
Placement Key: a–above; b–below; c–center; l–left; r–right; t–top.

ALAMY IMAGES: Pat Behnke 38tr; David Crausby 107tl; Directphoto. org 87tl; F. Jack Jackson 106tr; Panorama Stock/Li Jiangshu 98tl; Matthew Wellings 34tr; ALOFT HOTEL: 114tr; ASIA MEDIA: 60tl; CENTRO: 62tr; CORBIS: Arcaid/ Marcel Lam 40tl; Bettmann 33r; Burstein Collection 32tl; Hulton-Deutsch Collection 32tc; Kelly-Mooney Photography 12bc; Liu Liqun 99t; Reuters 35bl; FU FAMILY TEAHOUSE: 82tr; GETTY IMAGES: Cancan Chu 77tl; ChinaFotoPress/ Ma Wenxiao 40tr; Paul Gilham 33bl; Hulton 32c; The Image Bank/Andrea Pistolesi 8-9; Photographer's Choice/John Warden 28br; Taxi / Walter Bibikow 4–5; HATSUNE: 89tl; IBERIA CENTER FOR CONTEMPORARY ART: 25clb; IMAGINECHINA: Wu Changquing 26-27; Long Hai 38br; KEMPINSKI HOTELS: 29t, 112tl; LEONARDO MEDIA LTD.:114tl; MAI BAR: 82tl; MESH RESTAURANT: 3tc, 63bl; MIGAS RESTAURANT: 62tc; MOSTO: 61tl; PARK HYATT BEIJING: 113tl; PHOTOLIBRARY: Cash Cash 36tc; S Tauqueur 42tl, 90cr; PHOTOS12.COM: Panoramic Stock 28–9; RED GATE GALLERY: 84tr.; SCI-TECH HOTEL: 115tl; STUDIO PEI-ZHU: Liu Wentian 40br; TEMPLE RESTAURANT: 60cl; TEMPLESIDE HOUSE HOSTEL: 117tl; ULLENS CENTER FOR CONTEMPORARY ART: Fang Lijun 24-25c.

All other images are © Dorling Kindersley. For more information see *www.dkimages. com.*